Testimonials

C000063233

Praise for Tracy's Book

Ideas – this book is absolutely crammed full of them – and emotionally it really caught me. Great inspiration for readers!

Susan Quilliam,
Relationship Psychologist and
Agony Aunt for: AOL.co.uk; That's Life Magazine and Top Sante.
www.susanquilliam.com

I have to say that I think this is about the best book, of it's type, that I have come across. You are an inspiration!

Jaqetta Trueman, Designer, Wake the Tiger
www.wakethetiger.com

Reading your book, and talking to you has played a big part in helping me to take the plunge to find a new job and to go back home to Germany. I also quit smoking. Thanks for the push! Thanks for the inspiration!

Ira Hanenberg, Vetinary Surgeon

Written from the heart and with some fantastic insights for the reader. It's brilliant! This book definitely needs to be published!

Angela Sherman, Website Content/Copywriter
www.content-creation.co.uk

I love the book, very inspirational and motivational. Full of great insights and strategies to help anyone overcome limiting beliefs and live life to the full.

John Hotowka, After dinner Speaker/Magician
www.atouchofmagic.co.uk

If you want some tools and techniques to alter the course of your life, you will find them here. Not only that, Tracy's story will inspire you to get on with it NOW!

Mo Shapiro, Broadcaster, Author, Motivational Speaker.
www.inform-global.com

It's just what I've been looking for! Your message has really spurred me on. You've inspired me to tackle a fear that has stood in my way for a long time and shown me exactly how to do it. A benefit that I didn't expect is the catalyst it has given me to take my business to a whole new level.

Richard Duszczak, Cartoonist, Caricaturist and Illustrator.
www.cartoonstudio.co.uk
www.cartoonstudios.eng.net

Thank you SO much for sending me through more of your b ook. What a fantastic story!

Kate Bacon – Personal Coach, Pier To Peer Coaching
www.katebacon.co.uk

Testimonials

Praise for Tracy's Speaking Presentations

It was more than I could have hoped for. Absolutely superb! So motivational, so different; you went down a storm, very well done indeed!

I've done far more than I would have done without that session. I've found out about the cricket matches in Australia for December and started to look into flight details.

I'm meeting with the other regional teams in February. I'm going to talk to them about what we got out of it and suggest it for them.

Tim Roache, GMB, Britain's General Union

Tracy, there are only two speakers who I have seen score 9/10 from every delegate in the room. They score based on what they got out of it, and the quality of how they can use the information in their lives. Well Done!

Jeff Monks, Chairman of Groups for The Academy of Chief Executives

Tracy you were fantastic, the feedback has been tremendous. I am certainly going to make some changes in my own life as a result.

Jacqui Kavanagh, Meeting Planners International (UK)

I knew you'd be good but I wasn't prepared for that. You blew me away. You've really turned my life around. Thank you!

Lee Clarke, President
Bristol Chapter Professional Speakers Association & Financial Consultant

I thought you were excellent, I got a lot out of it. I've realised that if I really am going to get on with this speaking lark, I've just got to jolly well get on with it.

Tony Gordon, Financial Consultant and International Speaker

Well done with your speech. It was the first time that I have heard the 'famous' piano speech and I was really impressed—a great story, a great message also.

Martin Palethorpe, Peak Performance Coach & Speaker

I'm sitting here listening to Chopin while I mark assignments and thinking of you! I've decided I'm going to cycle the 'end to end' next year (Land's End to J O'Groats). That's my piano. Or one of them...

Naomi Crosby, Life Coach, Derby

May I thank you for putting across such an inspirational message. Your style is a winner!

Christa Spencer, DowHaltermann, Teeside, UK

Face the Music
and Win!

Tracy Plaice

**brave
press**

Face the Music and Win!

First published in 2006 by Brave Press
Magna House
East Leake
Leicestershire
LE12 6NJ

www.bravepress.com

ISBN 0-9553732-0-4
ISBN 978-0-9553732-0-6

Front cover design: Pat Ross, MMDesign, www.mmdesign.co.uk
Back cover wording & design: Graham Parker, Parker Communications,
www.parkercommunications.co.uk
Cover photography: Glen Tillyard, www.glentillyard.co.uk
Cartoon Illustration: Richard Duszczak, Cartoon Studio Ltd,
www.cartoonstudio.co.uk
Text layout design: Jaquetta Trueman, Graphic Solutions. www.wakethetiger.com

Printed and Bound by Lightning Source UK and USA

Acknowledgements

Writing this book has taken me on a rollercoaster ride of learning. The lessons that I learnt whilst conquering my fear with respect to playing a piano, have been put to good use again and again in this project.

There have been many people who have helped to bring this book to life. I would like to personally acknowledge those who helped.

I would like to thank my parents for giving me a musical education when I was young (among so many other things). I know that they worked very hard to provide me and my sister with as much as they could.

I would like to thank Mrs Hind – my first piano teacher, for spotting my passion for music and for giving me the opportunity to learn to play.

Many friends have created a much valued solid foundation of belief and support, as well as reading and giving feedback on the text. My thanks go especially to Mo Shapiro, Becky Knott, Angela Sherman, Ira Hanenberg, Helen Cassiday, John Hotowka, and Trupti Pandit. Thank you for being great friends!

I would also like to thank those who have added to the richness of the text with their comments and suggestions – Henry Hopking, Dominic Alldis, Gareth Chick, Lisa Jeavons, Jim and Jean Roberts, Ian and Ania Roberts.

The illustrations in this book have beautifully captured the essence of my story and I owe a huge vote of thanks to Richard Duszczak of Cartoon Motivators for his brilliant work. Thank you for bringing the ideas to life with such flair! Thanks also to John Hotowka for brainstorming the initial ideas with me.

In the story within the pages of the book, there are many people who I mention. They have provided places to play a piano, concerts in which to perform, resources that have helped me to make progress, ears to listen to a performance, and guidance in how to make the best use of my skills. Special thanks to every one of you!

The process of editing and getting the text ready to print has been one of the toughest jobs of all from my perspective, and I would like to thank Lesley Morrisey, Jo Parfit, LyAnn Petersen, and Jaquetta Trueman for their patience, diplomacy, and valuable contributions in this area.

There are others who have seen greater potential than I saw myself and challenged me to step up to their mark. For this gift I would like to thank Mo Shapiro, Steve McDermott, Jeff Monks, Martin Carver, and Maria Yugina.

I would like to thank Jana Stanfield for her inspiration to turn my life experience and passion for the piano into a keynote presentation. Also to thank Max Dixon for the fundamental part that he played with regard to finding my speaking message.

Within the membership of the Professional Speakers Association I have found unlimited abundance of encouragement and opportunity to grow. Thank you to all of you for sharing your wisdom and expertise.

My thanks too go to Richard Shardlow for listening when the going got tough, and keeping me fed when I didn't have patience to plan for it myself.

To all of you who have made a difference. Thank you very much!

Contents

Introduction

Why I Just HAD to Write This Book

You gain strength, courage and confidence by every experience in which you really stop to look fear in the face.

Eleanor Roosevelt

I had a passion as a youngster – it was playing a piano, but for many years fear got in the way of being able to share that passion with other people. Sixteen years of telling myself that one day I would get back to it, became a source of deep regret following an almost fatal car crash and a badly broken right hand.

That life-changing event became the catalyst that propelled me to take action. It left me with a burning desire to pack as much into the rest of my life as I could. I vowed to live every day to its fullest, to no longer put things off and to no longer limit what I was going to do because of feelings of fear. Physically, I was determined that my hand would recover so that I could play a piano again. Mentally, I was single-minded about learning how to quash the fear that had held me back.

With dogged determination and a whole host of methods of attack, within a year of starting to take action, I transformed from someone too scared to play for her own parents, to someone who had performed a solo piano piece in seven different concerts, culminating with an international performance.

As a direct effect, amazingly positive results have transpired across the whole of my life, discovering potential way beyond what I thought I had. With clear evidence that these methods work, I want to share them with anyone else who has the courage to make use of them, as I know that there are so many other people out there who really want something, but fear and 'reasons' keep getting in the way.

The 'reasons' why we don't take action are many – 'Not enough time' and 'Not enough money' I am sure come high on most people's list. I believe that often what lies buried behind these 'reasons' is fear of failure. So rather than try something and risk it not working out, we justify the inaction and commiserate ourselves with thoughts like - it wouldn't have worked out anyway.

Another major reason for writing this book is to save you the wait. I don't want you to have to experience a life-threatening event before you find the courage and determination to go after what you really want. It is my intention that through the pages of this book, you will find motivation and a route to success without the need for tragedy to leave you with regrets or spur you on once you have even more obstacles to overcome. My goal is to prompt you to take a closer look at your life, and to fire your imagination to consider what might be possible if you were willing to follow your passion beyond the confines of your comfort zone, beyond life's obstacles that will never go away.

Let me show you how, by pursuing something you are really passionate about, and pushing your skills beyond where you perceive your boundaries to be, you too can discover more of your true potential.

This book is for all of you out there who, when faced with a situation that induces the all-too-recognisable fluttering stomach, sweaty hands, and confused mind, you either avoid it or simply walk away. It's for those of you who have always wanted to do something, but are still waiting for the 'right moment' to come along. It is for those of you who may be behind a reception desk of a company, when you are capable of being on the board. It is for those of you who find yourself in an unhappy situation, but are too scared, or too stuck in a rut to do some thing constructive about it.

I want to give you a glimpse of what life might be like if you dared to take a leap of faith and go for what you truly desire. I'm going to show you how to become a risk taker rather than a risk avoider, and how to walk through 'the reasons' with your head held high, ready to embark on your next challenge. I want to save you years of wasted potential and empty promises to yourself.

Look at our society. How many people die of diseases induced by stress, a stress that was probably borne out of fear? Why aren't we taught how to deal with such destructive emotions when we are children? Why is it something we have to discover for ourselves?

Can you imagine what might happen if everyone was left to figure out how to drive a car on their own, without the guidance of someone experienced? There would be chaos on the road. Our rules are such that we have to seek advice from someone qualified to teach us. Well, imagine what might happen if we were similarly taught how to handle and conquer fear. It would have a huge impact across the whole of our lives.

Of course some fears are healthy; they stop us from putting our lives at risk and getting run over by traffic. However, most of the fear that stops us is just a perceived threat, not a real danger. It is an automatic response system in our bodies that clouds the judgement of our minds.

I'm sure that parts of my story will be familiar to you. Some of you may have been through much worse scenarios, while others may not have had anything drastic happen at all. But no matter which side of that divide you stand, I am sure there will have been times when you've allowed fear to prevent you from doing something you really wanted to do. We've all been there countless times and used the phrase, 'One day I'm going to...' Often it takes a tragedy or a health scare for us to realise that we may not have forever to 'get around to it.'

All around me I see so many people who stay firmly in their comfort zones and never venture out because of fear. Fear affects every aspect of our lives. How many people do you know who are too scared to leave a job even though they are not happy, because they are afraid they won't find another? Do you know people who are stuck in an unhappy relationship because they are too scared to go it alone? How many people settle for mediocrity, fearing that following a dream will lead only to hard work, disappointment and heartache? This kind of fear is the cause of so much frustration and wasted potential. It saddens me.

Through sharing my story I hope to inspire you and show you how to create a bolder, more productive version of yourself. If you choose to shape your life and follow the steps that I took (and am still taking), you'll be able to indulge and enjoy the passions in your life, expanding your sense of fulfilment and creating more opportunities for your future.

Years ago I read a quote that has stuck in my mind:

> *God had a great sense of humour, to have hidden*
> *our greatest talents where we most fear to tread.*

I know that certainly holds true for me. Would you be willing to see if it fits you too?

I travelled to the other side of the world to 'discover myself,' but, in fact, learnt the greatest lessons at the end of my finger-tips, playing a piano. Many people, from all walks of life ask me how I did it. I share those techniques through the pages of this book and through the presentations that I give, so that you too, will know how to step more boldly into your future and into your true potential.

Many people wait until it's too late – I nearly did. Don't let that happen to you.

If I can do it, then so can you!

Tracy Plaice

1 | My Story

Adversity has the effect of eliciting talents which in prosperous circumstances would have lain dormant.

Horace, 65-68 BC

In Pursuit of A Passion

I had always wanted to play the piano and told my parents about it frequently. I was inspired by Bobby Crush on the Opportunity Knocks television programme, hosted by Hughie Green. He remained top of the talent contest for six weeks playing ragtime music on the piano. I was transfixed by his hands – they seemed to dance effortlessly over the keys without him having to look at where they were going. Hearing what sounded like lots of different tunes all combining to create one wonderful melody fascinated me. And I remember that pageboy haircut, so trendy at the time, bouncing around in time to the music. The tune that he played was *The Entertainer* by Scott Joplin, which became very well known after that show.

One Christmas morning, waiting to go downstairs with Mum and Dad to open the presents, I thought that this might finally be the year that I would have a piano. But for Christmas that year, my parents bought me a guitar.

I was grateful; I knew they had paid a lot of money for it. I went along for lessons at a local guitar shop and was eager to learn, but really, all I wanted was a piano. Mrs Hind was my music teacher at school. She offered to teach me to play the piano after listening to me play the guitar one afternoon. When I told my parents about her offer, I was finally told that a piano was beyond their means, which is why I'd been given a guitar in the first place. Mrs Hind didn't see that as a reason for me not to learn to play, so my lessons began in the school music room and I practised at break times in the school hall. When I got home each evening, I would scour the pages of our local newspaper – The Evening Post, looking for a cheap piano. Finally I found one for sale for £25.

We went to look at it; it was lovely shades of mahogany brown, with brass candlestick holders on either side. I thought it was perfect despite the chips along the edge of the keys, where the little three-year-old of the house used to run his toy cars up and down. That small fact did not detract one iota from its beauty for me. Mum and Dad agreed to buy the piano and it was delivered the next day.

My favourite time to play was when I had the house completely to myself, as that was the only time I felt completely at ease and didn't make any mistakes. The piano was like my best friend; I shared with it all my emotions, and in return, it taught me that I could achieve things that seemed impossible at first glance. I still recall how difficult it was in the beginning to play with both hands together, when they were doing completely different things.

Playing the piano in front of the other people was always a real drama for me. I even found it a bit of a challenge to play for my piano teacher. At home when no one could hear me, I could perform perfectly, but in front of anyone else, especially an examiner, I would invariably make a mess, freeze, or lose my place in the music – all three sometimes. It didn't get any easier, no matter how hard I tried.

There were times at home when I would practise on the piano and Dad would sit, pretending to read the newspaper. I knew he was really listening to me play. He knew that was the only thing he could do to stand any chance of hearing what I was up to. It's not that I was being selfish by not wanting to perform for people, I just couldn't do it.

I wasn't a shy child in other areas of my life. In fact, I would quite often find myself in trouble for opening my mouth before my brain had considered the consequences, especially around my teachers and my father. I was made to sit alone at school on several occasions because I wanted to talk to my friend in the next chair, rather than read books.

I think the reason why I was so fearful when it came to playing the piano for others, was because it was so important to me. I would practise every day after school. I had really high expectations, both of myself and of what I thought other people would expect of me, given all the practice that I did. Also, and perhaps more importantly, I didn't really appreciate that I was any good at it. I would always compare myself unfavourably to Mrs Hind's other pupil, Alan.

Alan was the same age as me and he could play in front of people. In fact, I remember being told that he played better when he had an audience. I never talked about my fear and frustration with my performance ability, and I never questioned whether it might have been possible to do something about it.

Memories of Mistakes and Humiliation

Sunday afternoons when I was ten years old, would invariably find me getting into trouble when I would ask for bread and jam rather than being grateful for the salad put on the table for tea. It would also be a time of dread because Dad was bound to ask me to play a tune on the piano in front everyone. He knew I hated playing for other people for fear of making a mistake. As a fellow adult now, it's easy to see the efforts of parents wanting their child to have an opportunity to shine, but, at the time, it was not a welcomed event.

One of the worst Sundays I recall, all my relatives were there, my Mum, Dad and sister Beverley, my Grandma, Grandpa, Aunty Margaret, Uncle Raymond, and my cousins Kate and Steve.

'Tracy, Beverley, play us a tune', came the request after lunch. My sister had taken up the piano after me. She sat down and dutifully and perfectly, played a simple piece of music. Then all eyes were on me.

I felt the muscles in my back tense up, my stomach folded into knots and I squirmed and tried to get out of it, but to no avail.

The pit of my stomach was churning, and all I could think about were the mistakes I was bound to make, how awful they would sound, and the fact that everyone would expect me to be so much better than the performance I was about to give. I hated feeling this way.

I sat down to play and did as I was told, stumbling my way through the music. After just a few bars, fear got the better of me and I froze. It was like someone had pulled the plug; my brain no longer felt connected to my fingers. I couldn't think straight. All I remember is an overwhelming feeling of absolute embarrassment. I wanted the ground to open up and swallow me and the piano stool – whole.

After that experience, whenever anyone asked me to play in public, that dreadful feeling instantly came back.

Considering all that, it's amazing that I got up to the top grade in my music exams (Grade 8), which is as high as you can go before taking professional exams. I never did quite get that last one though, as studying for 'A' levels meant that I didn't have enough time for schoolwork and piano exams.

I left home to go to college at the age of 19 and hardly played a piano again for sixteen years. I would see them around, but they were usually in public places. It felt like they were taunting me, saying, 'I bet you daren't play me!' And not wanting anyone to hear, in case of a mistake, I wouldn't play.

There was only one occasion up to that point, when I had played for an audience successfully, but only because I hadn't realised anyone was listening. I was fifteen at the time and a dancer in the Czuplak Ukrainian Folk Dance group, which was led by my maths teacher from school – Mr Czuplak. We were performing at the Royal Concert Hall in Nottingham. We took part in concerts all over the place, mainly in folk festivals around Europe, but that day we were performing in our home city. We had finished the dress rehearsal in the afternoon and everyone had disappeared to while away a couple of hours before we needed to get dressed for the concert. I hung around on the stage because in the wings, I had spotted a gleaming, full-size, black Steinway Grand Piano – one of the best brands you can buy in the piano world. I couldn't resist – when was I likely to get another opportunity to play such a beautiful instrument?

Convinced no one would hear me, I sat down to play one of my favourite tunes, *The Teddy Bears' Picnic*. As I finished I heard great applause. It was only then that I found out that the speakers on the stage were two-way, and they were relaying my performance throughout the theatre and straight into the dressing rooms where my friends were resting. My blush made beetroot pale by comparison!

My Career

Persistence begins at an early age and I know I needed lots of it with my exams at school. I re-sat three of my 'O' levels at age 16 and then repeated a whole year of 'A' levels at the age of 18, hoping to improve on the grades that had failed to get me into University to study the Accountancy degree I had my heart set on. My second attempt still didn't get me there, so I took an alternative path that eventually led me to work as an Optician.

I became interested in the field of vision after applying for a job as a Dispensing Optician between leaving school for the first time and re-sitting my 'A' levels. A Dispensing Optician is the person who fits your glasses once you have had a sight test. I was attracted because I had been wearing glasses myself since the age of fifteen. I didn't get the job, but talking to my own Optician about what his job involved planted a seed that gave me alternatives when I didn't get my first choice of career. So, at the age of 19, I left home and moved to London to study dispensing. My 'O' levels were all I needed to secure a place and at the time, I felt frustrated at the thought that I had just wasted three years of my life studying for 'A' levels.

Once I qualified as a Dispensing Optician at the age of twenty-one, I found a job with a small independent company in Hayes, Middlesex, and was fortunate to live in one of their flats above another shop in Northwood Hills – one of the smarter suburbs of North-West London.

Losing My Piano

Seven years after leaving home, my parents informed me they wanted to get rid of my old piano in favour of a sideboard. I had changed jobs and moved to the east end of London by this time, but I was still living in a first floor flat. I measured the space in the corridor around the stairwell, but it was too narrow for my piano to get through.

The issue lay down for a while, but I remember the phone call from my parents telling me the piano was advertised for sale with the reasoning, 'Well, you never play it for us anyway ...' A week later I had exhausted all the people I thought might be willing to take care of it for me until I found a place where I could keep it for myself. The call that came from Dad to say the piano was sold left me sobbing on the other end of the phone like a young child who had lost their favourite toy.

My Other Passion – Australia

As a child, every time my grandparents took us on holiday to Skegness, we would play on the beach and my Grandma would say, 'If you dig deep enough, you'll be able to go and see your Uncle Harold.'

My Grandma's brother had emigrated at the age of 16, to the Gold Coast in Queensland, Australia. I had met him only twice at my grandma's house over the years and heard all about the sea being warm enough for him to swim in every morning before he played a round of golf. From a very early age I knew all about kangaroos, koala bears and the Great Barrier Reef. I had always had a longing to see it for myself.

University at Last

At the age of twenty-four, I finally made it to University, thanks to a change in the entry requirements. My dispensing qualification and a subsequent contact lens qualification, plus my 'A' levels, (even though they were in irrelevant subjects), opened up a chance for me to study Optometry, which would lead to a job actually testing the eyes, rather than just dispensing the glasses and contact lenses. In the back of my mind I was thinking that this qualification might one day take me to Australia, as I knew that it was recognised out there.

I found the degree really hard work, especially when it came to the Chemistry aspect of the course. I didn't even have a basic 'O' level in the subject and I was studying beyond 'A' level in this area. I took time out from those subjects that I did know about, to devote more to those areas where my skills were lacking.

What made me really sad and angry at the system, was watching the frustrations of one of my fellow students who re-sat every year of our course and still didn't get through. He would go to pieces every time it came to written or oral exams. He was just as good at the subject as I was. Our only difference was that I was not as immobilised by the fear of scrutiny in this area as him. We all have chinks in our armour in different places. I understood very well from my piano experiences how debilitating and vexing this kind of fear could be. Yet, in all that time, no one took him aside and helped him to conquer this fear. I really felt for him. I heard that he actually joined another University and started again with a successful outcome. What grit and determination is that?! He could write his own book on the subject of persistence in following a passion. What a waste though of so much talent, and so much heart ache!

With regard to my Australian dream, my determination held and straight after qualifying, I applied for a job in the city of Melbourne. After a successful interview in London, I was offered a post that was to start in four months time. But during each phone call with my future employers, something about the terms of my contract would change: the money I would be paid, the time I was expected to stay, or the amount of holiday I was entitled to. I had a sense of foreboding about the position and didn't quite trust my new potential employers, so I eventually turned the offer down and put that dream to the back of my mind. I took up freelance work instead using contacts from my former days as a Dispensing Optician.

Five years later, and completely unexpectedly, the dream re-surfaced. At University, I had studied optometry with a girl called Trupti who had quickly become one of my best friends. We stayed in touch beyond the course and one day, out of the blue, she called me and said, "Tracy, I've quit my job, Sanjiv and I are going to live in Sydney and look for work once we get there. We've got student visas so we can work anywhere and I'm going to look for some freelance work as an Optician.".

Although I was happy for her, I was surprised at the strong pangs of jealousy that were suddenly rearing their heads. It was like rubbing salt in a wound. How could she do that before I had? She knew that was my dream. We'd spoken about it many times at University and she never said that she wanted to go too.

As Trupti was still under 30 years of age, she could apply for a visa that allowed her to work for anyone for up to three months. I, on the other hand, was now 32, and if I wanted to go, I would have to be sponsored and have a job to go to in order to secure a visa.

On the positive side, the call did give me a kick-start toward questioning how I might get out there too. Since I had put my dream aside, my circumstances had changed considerably. I was no longer the foot-loose girl I had been. I was married to Richard and had moved house to be nearer to my parents. I tried to reason with myself that uprooting now would be too difficult, that my husband wouldn't want to go, and that I should just let sleeping dogs lie, but it was no use. I knew I wanted to go. I started talking about it to test the water, but it was not favourably received or considered as a serious option.

As it turned out, Trupti found it more difficult to find work than expected and after three months, booked herself a round-the-world flight, opting to travel instead. One week after booking the ticket, she called and said, "Tracy, you'll never believe it, I've just been offered this great job in a place called Airlie Beach. It's the gateway to The Whitsundays, a beautiful place in north Queensland with a tropical rainforest, and 72 islands dotted off the coast. It's just a few miles off shore to the Great Barrier Reef. The contract's for a year. I can't take it ... do you want it?".

Within 30 minutes I had called the Australian Embassy about visas, called the Australian Optometry Board to request application forms for registration, and contacted the agency that had offered her the job. That day, I was so excited, living in the fantasy of my mind, that I completely forgot to call my husband to tell him about it.

That night, he got home before me. The agency called and the conversation began, "About your wife's job in Australia ..." Well, you can imagine the atmosphere when I got home. As I had expected, he was adamant and voiced all the reasons I had already told myself as to why we couldn't go – new house, new mortgage, new jobs, he didn't want to go, and my parents wouldn't want us to go. The list went on.

The next few weeks were a real challenge with our clashing views. I was determined not to let my dream die. I desperately wanted to seize the opportunity that had been laid before me. My salvation came three weeks later in the form of a holiday programme about The Whitsundays that Richard and I sat watching together. It showed the beautiful, idyllic white beaches, boats cruising in the blue ocean, people diving and exploring the colourful, tropical fish on the barrier reef, and talked about the idylic warm sunny climate. It was those images that finally made him turn to me and say, "OK, let's go!" So, one by one, we dealt with the 'reasons' for not going, and four months later we were living in Australia!

Living The Dream
Certainly from the point of living out my dream, our time in Australia was fantastic. I was waking up to sunshine every

morning and able to walk in the rainforest after work. I learnt to dive and sail and relished being there. What I hadn't anticipated though, was feeling frustrated in my work; the practice was very quiet and not busy enough to tax my brain, so I often found myself twiddling my thumbs and bored. I wasn't allowed to tackle other issues in the business, so I would often sit around reading or talking to the receptionist.

There was discord at home too, as Richard was frustrated by not being able to find work. It's amazing how the dynamics of a relationship can change dramatically when you don't have your usual pastimes, roles to play, and support systems around you. Eventually, when Richard trained as a diving instructor, this put us on a more even keel.

After a year, it had become obvious that there wasn't enough work for my boss and another Optician; so, by mutual consent we transferred my sponsorship. Richard and I thought that if we were going to move, we might as well see another part of the country, so I applied for a position with a company called For Eyes, in Perth, Western Australia.

In fact, things didn't pan out quite as we had hoped; still feeling frustrated at the situation and with the prospect of difficulty finding new work, Richard decided he would make the most of our overseas assignment and travel around the country. He told me via a phone call whilst I was back at home in the UK, visiting my parents. So I had no choice in the matter. He said he would join me at a later point once he had got some of the travel bug out of his system. I was very upset that he wanted to see the country without me, and envious that he had the freedom to roam whilst I was tied to my job. If I were to quit, I'd have had to relinquish the working business visa, meaning neither of us would be allowed to stay and work. So, once I was in Perth, I got on with creating a new home alone in a new place.

My contact with Richard over the phone was sporadic and constrained, as my feelings alternated between wanting to encourage him to live his dream, and being absolutely distraught that he was content to travel without me and that we weren't together. Three months later Richard called to say he had arrived in Perth.

The call came first thing in the morning as I was getting ready to leave for work. The air between us was fraught with tension, and we arranged to meet at lunchtime in the car park near my work. But my journey didn't follow its usual course that day.

The Crash

My route to work was along a really fast, open road. One of the trees that I would pass was adorned with silk flowers and had plaques with the names 'Colin' and 'Chloe' on it. Each day as I passed them, I would wonder about the lives that were cut tragically short and say a silent 'hello' to them.

I hadn't reached that point yet on this particular morning, when all of a sudden, a white van started to pull out from the side road to turn right directly in the path of my lane. I was travelling at the speed limit – almost 70 miles an hour, but time seemed to slow right down in those few moments; just like you see in the films when the action is in slow motion. The driver obviously hadn't looked; the van was only 20 metres in front of me.

I honestly thought I was about to die and take another person with me. In those few moments, I had time to think. It was like my life was laid clearly before me. For the last few months I had been existing rather than truly living – consumed by worry, fears and doubts, thinking about what might happen because of the dramas and separation of my marriage. What came to my mind were all the tears that I had shed, and what a waste of time it had been – living beneath a cloud of worry. Such a shame that fear had ruled the day.

As I approached the van, I wasn't scared, just quietly accepting of what was to be. I thought I was about to meet Colin and Chloe and, strangely enough, Princess Diana. I was conscious that if I hit the door of the van head-on, I would kill the person who was driving. I looked to the other side of the road – nothing was coming. I gripped the wheel, swerved to the right and braced myself against the steering wheel for the impact.

The Aftermath

When I came to and realised I was alive, my first thought was to get out of the car in case it was about to explode. I felt relief, disbelief and a searing pain in my right hand. A stranger at my door helped me out of my seat.

Walking towards me, clutching her right elbow, was the woman who had been driving the van. Through uncontrollable sobs, she was trying to apologise to me. I felt in a daze, apart from the searing pain in my hand, which was throbbing out of all proportion like that of a character in a cartoon. My clothes were bloodstained and the car was a wreck. As I looked back, I could hardly believe I had walked away alive. I found my phone and called work to let them know what had happened. As I spoke to Dee, my colleague, tears erupted and I remember wondering, 'Why am I crying? I'm alive, I'm OK.'

I had severe whiplash to my neck, I had hit my head on the window, my knee was bleeding where it had been bashed under the steering column, my jacket was torn, my stomach was sore from the seat-belt – but the only real problem that I was fully aware of, was my right hand.

X-rays at hospital revealed I had broken it right in the middle. All the supporting ligaments around my fingers had taken the brunt of the force of the impact, as I had gripped my hand so tightly around the steering wheel on impact. It was incredibly painful to move. I was devastated to think that for 16 years, I had been 'going to get around to' playing the piano again, and now I was facing the prospect that I might never be able to use my hand again, let alone play a piano.

The next few days were a blur. I needed lots of help to do everything. To add to the anguish, a call from Richard's brother in the UK informed us that his mother had been taken into hospital and was very sick. They couldn't tell us how serious it was, and we were unsure if Richard should stay and help me or fly home to see his Mum. Two days after the crash there was another call from his brother to ask Richard to get on a plane as soon as possible.

The next day at the airport, half an hour before his flight, we received the devastating news that his mother had passed away. It was awful watching Richard walk away in floods of tears about to endure a 24 hour flight knowing that he was too late. I wanted to be there to comfort him, but we hadn't been able to get two tickets to go together, so I flew home the following day.

There was a lot for Richard to organise at home with regard to the funeral and dealing with his mother's estate which was south of London. I was at home with my parents in the Midlands, three hours drive away. I had hospital appointments to keep to monitor progress of my broken hand and whip lash injuries. We were spending very little time together.

The Recovery

After six weeks back in the UK, I had to fly back to Perth to return to work if I was to keep the business visa. Richard had to remain in the UK to manage the sale of his mum's house.

My first morning back at work in Perth, the manager took me into the sight-test room at 9am and greeted me with the words, "Thanks to you, we've lost $30,000 in the last six weeks."

I couldn't believe that he was laying the blame at my feet. I could have died in the crash; the company car insurance they had covered the car, but not my livelihood. It wasn't my fault that replacement staff were so hard to come by. They could have used a locum agency. I had come back to Australia to work before I felt ready due to the badgering I had received from them over the phone. And with the emotional turmoil that had gone on in the meantime, with losing Richard's mum and being separated from him yet again, my feelings were very mixed. Part of me wanted to curl up and cry, and the other part wanted to punch him!

Going back to work was difficult. My hand wasn't working properly and was very sore. Not being able to freely use both hands was frustrating. The year that followed seemed to consist of an endless stream of visits to the hand surgeon, the physiotherapist, the chiropractor, the counsellor and the solicitor. I was alone for another four months before Richard could join me. It was not an easy time.

Before the crash, my favourite pastime which kept me fit and provided me with an opportunity to meet new people, had been Ceroc dancing (a partner dance that looks a bit like jive but is danced to modern day dance tracks). With my right hand in the state it was, that was out of the question. Even basic functions that I had taken for granted were proving to be a problem. I even had trouble lifting a mug for the first few months after my plaster came off. I would drop things unexpectedly and not understand how it had happened. I didn't get any warning that I couldn't hold onto something, it would just fall.

The job of an Optician requires good dexterity with both hands. Not being able to use one of them properly was very frustrating. I became thoroughly depressed. Even though I was having counselling, the seemingly endless appointments to all the different consultants made me feel like a hamster on a wheel, going nowhere. I remember sitting on the end of my bed sobbing at 3 o'clock one morning and calling home. Through tears I spoke to Dad who assured me that I could always come home, but I was a stubborn mule and didn't want to give in to circumstances.

Sometimes you have to reach rock bottom before you can take the steps to change your life. This was definitely one of those points for me.

Preserving My Sanity

The one hobby that I could still pursue, and one that probably preserved my sanity, was Toastmasters. It was through this group that I discovered a real passion for public speaking. I had discovered the organisation when we lived in Airlie Beach. Toastmasters is a global organisation that teaches people the skills of public speaking. I remember thinking at the first meeting that if I could speak well in public, then I should be able to use those same skills one day to play a piano in public too.

I had promised myself that my tenth speech would include a piano performance. As it turned out, by the time I came to give that tenth speech, I hadn't taken any steps to find a piano to practise on, I had moved to Perth and I had survived a car crash. I was still having physiotherapy three times a week, and did not have full use of my right hand. Instead of a piano performance, I gave a presentation called, *Live Your Dream – Don't Dream Your Life*. I had felt the urge to write it after watching the destruction of the events of September 11th in New York. It was about following your passion and not waiting until it was too late. So began my first keynote speech.

I was absolutely determined that my hand was going to re-cover and I WAS going to play a piano and conquer the fear that had stopped me from sharing my passion for music with other people. I am determined by nature, but the levels I have gone to in pursuit of playing a piano have surprised even me.

Having the car crash and realising that life might have come to an end, was like putting rocket fuel in my petrol tank, as far as determination was concerned. It helped me to focus my sights beyond the painful hours spent in physiotherapy with a practitioner bending my fingers at an angle that they no longer seemed physically able to go.

I didn't start out with any particular strategy in mind for conquering my fear. I was just constantly on the lookout for how I could challenge my mind and my body to go beyond my perceived limits.

There were many things that I did to conquer my fear and move beyond those 'reasons.'

What follows in the rest of this book describes how each of the actions I took played a part in effecting a big change. Basically, I took myself on – mind, body and soul. The strategies I used involved lots of action steps supported by many networks of people and resources. As you read on, I want you to think about how you might use the ideas and tactics in pursuit of your own passion – mine's playing the piano, what's yours?

2 | Speak Up!

If the creator had a purpose in equipping us with a neck he surely meant for us to stick it out!

Arthur Koestler

I have always been known for speaking my mind, and some people say I have the cheek of the devil. But my view is that the more people who know what I want to achieve, the more likely I am to get there!

When you have helping hands and hearts in pursuit of your goal, the ride is much smoother, quicker, and easier than going it alone.

What inspires me about children is their ability to ask for what they want. They have no concept of what should and should not be shared – often to the embarrassment of their parents. It's a quality that is ground out of us as we repeatedly hear comments like:

> *'I want, never gets!'*

> *'Speak when you're spoken to!'*

> *'You can't always have everything you want!'*

I discovered that talking about my quest to conquer my fear of playing the piano in public was like unlocking a treasure trove. It led to all sorts of opportunities and resources that helped me en route to success.

People told me about all manner of things that they were scared of – how they had conquered their fears, how their lives had changed as a result, and what they were passionate about. I was also offered suggestions for books that might help me, useful websites to refer to, details for contacting people with relevant skills, and much more. The more people I spoke to, the more opportunities appeared before me.

Tell The World

There are many benefits from letting the world know what you are up to.

I think what stops us speaking to others about our passion is often a feeling that people won't be interested, or we are afraid to ask for help in case the response is 'no.' What I have learnt is that often, a 'no' is followed by, 'but I know a person who can'. So ultimately, the 'no' still takes me one step closer to where I want to go.

When people buy into your purpose and your 'reason why' you want to achieve something, many of them will want to help.

Putting an advert out into the world about what you want will:

- Allow other people to think about how they might help you – most people love to make a difference. If you let them contribute a little along the way, it will make you both feel good.

- Create a source of ideas from other people that you might never have thought of.

- Help you to find others on a similar quest.

- Help you to find people with specialist knowledge.

- Lead you to all sorts of resources that you may not have found alone.

- Keep your progress in perspective as others admire your courage.

- Tell your subconscious that you mean business and are serious about your intentions.

Think of it like this: you are shipwrecked on an island and no one knows you are there. So how do you get the message out that you want help?

Consider that every time you open your mouth to share with another human being what it is that you want to achieve, you are throwing a 'message in a bottle' into the sea of life. You may have no idea who will get to hear your plea, but you can be sure that if you don't throw your message into the sea in the first place, you will have no chance of finding that someone who can help you.

The concept of networking has sprouted a prolific number of groups across the globe whose main aim is to share information, ideas and business contacts in order to help people reach their goals. They do this not only for business goals, but for personal goals too.

Be The Match-Maker For Other People

Ecademy is one of the most successful of these networking groups which started via the internet from the UK, but has since become global and attracts a vast number of members from all over the world. This book was almost complete when I heard one of the co-founders – Thomas Power; give a presentation about why he did it and what has worked really well for him. He touched on points that I hadn't emphasized so much in my own work, but which I felt were really pertinent to include. He reminded us of the importance of giving to others before we expect to receive. That often, we can get a better result by giving connections rather than by asking for them. I believe there is value in knowing how to do both.

Thomas told us the three questions that have most successfully helped him to build rapport and make connections for others when meeting at networking events:

1. What is your area of expertise?

2. What's the biggest project that you are working on right now?

3. Who can I put you in touch with that can help you with that project?

Remember that there are only six degrees of separation between you and anyone in the world. In other words, you can reach EVERYONE in the world in no more than six connections. This means you know someone who – through their network – can connect with someone else – who will use their network to connect with someone … and so on. But it won't take more than six people in the chain before you reach the person you want.

You never know who your friends, family and business contacts already know, and where your next lead might come from to help you make progress. The more people that you help and the more people who know what you are looking for, the more opportunities you create for help to come your way.

A Source of Inspiration

We hear plenty of stories in the news about things going wrong in the world, but rarely are we fed stories of inspiration that give us hope about our own ability to achieve. When you talk to other people about what you are up to, and provide them with an opportunity to help you on your way, you are likely to become a source of inspiration to others.

If praise comes your way as a result, learn to accept it graciously. It can help to keep your progress in perspective making you less likely to mentally beat yourself up for not being further along the road than you think you should be.

If as a result of this kind of conversation, other people are spurred on their way too, then all the better! It can be a fantastic source of inspiration and energy back to you when others relate what they have done as a result of speaking to you.

So don't be shy, share your progress and share the opportunity to make a difference!

A Source of Creative Thinking

Scientists tell us that our conscious mind represents only 8% of our total brain capacity. The language we use to talk about an issue sends a clear signal to our subconscious. It then goes to work to figure out how to solve that problem when we are not aware of it. That is often the reason why our best ideas for solutions come to us in a flash when we are doing something completely unrelated.

So you can see why it's really important that you talk about what you want to achieve. It's sending that message to your subconscious all the time, helping you to build the level of belief that will assist you in reaching your objective and helping you to find others who can steer you in the right direction along the way.

Learning How to Speak Up

I mentioned my involvement with Toastmasters briefly in Chapter 1. My introduction to this organisation was prompted by an invitation from one of my patients when I was working as an Optician in North Queensland, Australia.

The first meeting I went to was in Bowen, one hour north of where we were living in Airlie Beach. I went out of curiosity and thought it would be a good way to meet the locals.

The format of the meeting really intrigued me. The presentations changed every five minutes and were about all manner of things. It was obvious that some of the speakers were battling hard with their nerves. I felt privileged to see such courage and determination in action.

Over the weeks I saw those speakers grow in confidence as their skills took root and blossomed. The presentations offered great insight into their lives, and the members soon began to feel like family, which, being so far away from home, filled a big hole for me.

The first manual that I worked through was called The Competent Toastmaster. The ten speeches in that manual cover the basics of speech structure, the use of humour, props, creative us e of language and, towards the end, focus on how to motivate and inspire your audience.

I loved putting pen to paper in preparation for all of these. I found myself researching and allowing my inquisitive nature to come back, reminiscent of my days at University. After giving a speech, what would be a real thrill for me was to have someone come up and say that I'd made them think, and have them tell me what they were going to do as a direct result of listening.

This still gives me a buzz when I speak to audiences today. It's the thrill of planting a seed and imagining what great tree might grow out of it that keeps me coming back for more.

The interesting thing about Toastmasters is that the people who go along are ordinary people like you and me. They're not all people who have to give presentations in their line of work. The skills that you acquire make conversation on a one-to-one basis more free-flowing, as well as helping you to learn how to present before an audience. For many people it's a hobby that is fun and boosts self-confidence.

When I moved to Perth in Western Australia I continued with Toastmasters, and I took it one stage further when my interest was caught by an advert for a seminar called, 'Speak for Money', hosted by the National Speakers Association of Australia (NSAA). This organisation offered both education and a community for those professionals who speak for a living. I went to that training day and also to their monthly chapter meeting. I was so inspired by the people I met. There were experts from the worlds of finance, business planning, marketing, internet technology, writing – the list went on. The standard of their presentations was fantastic. I was so impressed by this, and the knowledge that they shared about how to build a speaking career, that I signed up for their annual convention in Adelaide after just one meeting. I had gained a sneak preview into a whole new world, and I wondered if there could be a possible career somewhere in it for me.

At that time, I had no idea what my topic or expertise could be, I just knew that these people really sparked a feeling of determination and drive within me. In my experience it is rare to find so many people so passionate about their work, so generous in sharing their methods of success, and so excited about the difference they make in other people's lives. I wanted to be around people like them.

I knew from my work and from how my speeches were received at Toastmasters that I was effective with my communication skills. I had never analysed in great detail how or why my language was considered 'engaging,' until I started attending self-development courses.

Self-Development Courses
One of those courses was called 'Communication Performance and Power' and was led by an organisation called Landmark Education. I took my first steps in the arena of public piano performance as part of this.

I was in Melbourne at the time, having resigned from my job in Perth in favour of doing what I truly wanted – to travel around Australia in a camper van so that I could finally see the country.

There were over a hundred people on the course. We received coaching and guidance in all sorts of areas. These ranged from how we relate to ourselves, to what it is that we think we are capable of achieving. We looked at how to let go of our 'reasons from the past' that keep us trapped in a pattern of reactive behaviour. Learning about communication and how to be effective in our conversations had a big impact on me.

We were coached in the art of speaking in public in a way that would grab people's attention whilst being really clear about our message and request. We were taught how to speak in terms of what had held us back, the vision we had, and what it was that we needed help with to take us to the next level.

The transformation in the way people and their stories came across was amazing. You can imagine that, in front of an audience of a hundred or so, not too many people had their hands up volunteering to be coached at the beginning. As the hours passed by, people could see that the benefit massively outweighed the feelings of fear, and so the queue for the microphone grew. It was a fantastic learning opportunity. The safe and confidential environment meant that, by the end of the course, almost everyone had chosen to spend time being coached or to share stories and personal insights.

After two days we were set a challenge to achieve something really significant in our lives – whether it was achieving a goal, putting a relationship back on track, or clearing something up.

Until then, I had only ever reached the 'wishful thinking' stage with respect to my goal of conquering my fear of playing a piano in public. That was the point when I resolved that, between the Sunday night, when we were being set the challenge, and Thursday evening, when we were all going to come together again, I would perform in public playing the piano – three times.

I hadn't played for sixteen years; my hand was now healed, but stiff and a bit on the weak side. I was in a city where I knew no one, apart from the people I had sat in the course with over the weekend, and I was staying in my camper van on a caravan site. Pianos aren't standard kit in those sorts of places!

Putting The Learning Into Practice
Not having a piano is not a valid excuse for not being able to play one!
Having decided on our goals, the chairs were moved out of the way to enable us to move around the room to tell at least five other people what we wanted to achieve. My story was told,

my objective shared and I asked them if they could help me find somewhere to practise the piano. The fourth person that I spoke to was called Danny. His response to my story and request was just what I was looking for:

"Tania, my wife, is a piano teacher. She's over there – I'm sure you could come and practise at our house," he said.

For the next three days I visited their home each morning. I had to catch two different trams to get there, as I just couldn't face driving the camper van, with its restricted visibility and lack of power-steering, through the unfamiliar, busy streets of Melbourne.

Practising at Tania's house felt great! I hadn't realised how much I had missed playing the piano and the sense of joy and calmness that it gave me. Each morning I practised for one and a half hours. I was proud that I was finally taking some action rather than just talking about it.

Tania and Danny's house was very grand. The piano room had a beautifully edged high ceiling with a central chandelier. The far wall was lined from floor to ceiling with a wooden bookcase, and there was a huge bay window that let in loads of light.

The house was big enough that Tania didn't have to sit with me while I played, so I could forget about the fact that she could hear me. Well, sort of ... when I first started playing I put the damper pedal on, which cuts the volume by a third, so I couldn't be heard easily!

As was to be expected, after a while Tania ventured in, wanting to hear what I was playing. The instant familiar tension came across my back, and I had to beat down the feelings of trepidation and fear of making a mistake.

I was conscious that as a teacher, Tania was aware of the standard I should be capable of, having studied up to grade 8. Ignoring the derogatory self-talk that said, 'I can't play in front of people,' I fumbled my way through the piece of music. It was frustrating (but not unfamiliar) to not be able to play as well with her in the room. I just kept reminding myself how lucky I was to be alive, and that my hand had recovered to such a point that the pain no longer stopped me from using it.

I was glad that I had my favourite piano music with me. The bright pink folder containing my music had been one of the things I'd packed when I left the UK for Australia. It had always been my intention to do something with it but, for over three years, it had been tucked away in a box, unused. It was a victim to the sentence, 'I'll get around to it.'

My right hand felt sore from the practice, especially along the knuckles. I could feel tension along my forearms, and the whiplash injuries in my neck came back to remind me that they hadn't fully healed yet. Considering what I'd been through with the car crash and how long it had been since I'd played a piano, it wasn't really a surprise to feel discomfort whilst practising. The enthusiasm and commitment that I felt helped to take me beyond the mental and physical challenges.

My piano skills were rusty, my hand was sore, but it felt GREAT that I was finally doing something about conquering my fear and getting back to my passion.

Tania had reassured me that the layers of rust would fall away easily, and on the third day, she said that she could hear a vast improvement. I had even inspired her to play more for herself. She told me that she could see, from watching me take so much joy from practising, that she had lost some of the sense of fun and enjoyment that she used to feel and how her view had narrowed to that of a 'teacher' rather than a student.

Taking action is not always easy, but if you take one step at a time, you'll find you're soon moving in the direction of your goal.

First Steps

Of course, practising isn't performing – even though with Tania watching, it sometimes felt like it. I still had to find my three opportunities to perform in public.

Each afternoon I would put my tourist hat back on and take in the sights of Melbourne, keeping in mind the question – where can I perform? My first opportunity came as I was shopping for music one afternoon. A haunting tune had caught my attention earlier in the week as I sat in a café. I found out from the waitress that it was a piece called *Gymnopedie No 1* by Erik Satie, and I had set out to buy myself a copy.

The music shop had an amazing display of pianos. At the back, there were three gleaming, black Steinway baby grand pianos up on a platform, under spotlights, with full-length mirrors behind them. The cheapest was A$26,000 – that's about £10,500. I thought that was a good enough place for my performances to start.

I explained to the girls behind the desk my story about wanting to conquer my fear by facing it, and asked permission to play. The staff smiled back at me and said it was OK. I pulled out my pink folder, put the music for *Love Story* on the stand, took a deep breath and began. As I finished, the female assistant who had served me clapped and smiled via the mirrors on the wall. She was now standing behind me.

With a kind smile and a sparkle in her eye, she warned me that I could get into trouble for using photocopies of music when performing in public. I asked if she played. She told me that she was a music student and earned a bit of money by performing. I asked if she could play the piece by Satie that I had just bought.

She sat down to play it for me. It was beautiful! The music floats you on a cloud in a trance-like way. I loved the grace with which her left hand struck a note down at the far end of the keys and then, with great poise and elegance, was lifted high in the air, moving halfway up the keyboard and perfectly striking the next note without her even looking to see where her hand was going. That is one of the things about playing a piano that has always fascinated me. I used to question, how people did that. Having mastered the art myself, I can answer that it's like learning a very precise high jump for the hands, and I feel proud that I can now do that too.

The opportunity for my second performance came as I was taking my friend David shopping for glasses – putting my op-tometry skills to good use.

Having arrived at the Optician's before it was open, we de-cided to browse around the open shopping mall. As fate would have it, right in the centre of this huge complex was a display of the latest digital pianos. Perfect, I thought, for performance number two.

After I played *Love Story* (yet again), I decided to play with the gadgets – these were no ordinary pianos. These had classical tunes recorded in the memory, and there was even a function to allow you to play the tunes yourself guided by lights that lit up the relevant keys, showing you which notes to hit next. There were 'easy', 'medium' and 'difficult' settings. I scrolled down the list and found the Satie piece, so just one day after buying the music, I was able to play the 'difficult' version note perfect, performing in the centre of a huge shopping mall – brilliant!

Opportunity three came through Alvin, who was one of the five people I had shared my quest with on the course. He told me about his 15-year-old daughter, who had learnt to play the piano, but now, having reached grade 5, was considering giving it up. I told Alvin that I would like to play for his daughter as one of my performances.

Although it didn't happen until the Sunday after the course had finished, the commitment and time were in place by the time the group reconvened on the Thursday.

That following Sunday, we went to a restaurant that had been created from a former prison. The original layout, with the galleried landings and a view from the central floor right up to the skylight on the ceiling, was still clearly visible. There was a piano on the first level, on a balcony, just above the restaurant area. It was a gleaming, white baby grand.

The restaurant was packed with people enjoying their Sunday morning breakfast, and we asked permission from the maitre d', and the restaurant manager to play. They were delighted to see the piano played. I was very nervous. 'They won't want their breakfast disturbed by me,' I thought. I just had to keep reminding myself that this wasn't about me and how many mistakes I might make – it was about Alvin's daughter and my desire to inspire her enough to think carefully about her decision to give up playing. I didn't necessarily want to change her mind, but I wanted her to understand what a gift it is to be able to play for yourself and to be able to share that with other people. I had always admired those people who could and would share their passion for music, and so it was my turn to join them rather than being the one always watching with envy.

Inevitably, I played *Love Story*, as well as another piece that my first music teacher had often played for me, that being *Robin's Return* by Fisher. I could feel myself shaking with fear.

I don't even remember if I received any applause or not – all I remember is how glad I was when the whole thing was over. I also recall Alvin's daughter beaming at me as I finished.

A year later, I received an email from Alvin telling me that his daughter had just passed grade 6!

Returning to the Thursday evening event at the Landmark Education building, I was incredibly proud of what I had achieved in such a short space of time. The stories from the other participants were just as forthright and bold:

- One man had organised a charity golf event in four days and had convinced celebrities from America to be a part of it. He had even arranged TV coverage.

- One young girl had written a song, which she performed, accompanied by her guitar. We had to wait a few seconds each time she had to change chords and move her fingers, but her passion and willingness to share despite her not being that proficient had tears rolling down my cheeks. The lyrics were beautiful and made your heart swell at how great and varied life is.

The other stories from people blur into my memory, but what was very apparent was that when you knock down every perceived barrier and limiting belief, it is amazing what you can achieve. I had a real sense of excitement thinking, 'If I can achieve that in a week, what will be possible in a year?'

Keep The Momentum Going
Having learnt to 'fake it', at least as far as nerves were concerned, in front of three different audiences, I continued to push the boundaries. I was hungry for results and evidence that I was making progress.

A month later, and now in Adelaide, I attended that annual convention for the National Speakers Association of Australia which I mentioned earlier. Seeing top professional speakers in action once again was amazing. There was one speaker in particular who really gave me food for thought. Jana Stanfield conveyed a very inspiring message through the words of the songs she had written, and by telling stories about her life. Accompanied by her guitar, she held the audience spellbound and moved me to tears when she spoke about family members that had been loved and lost. Her keynote left me with a renewed sense of wonder and intrigue about the twists and turns in life that can feel overwhelming at times. I particularly liked the chorus of the tune that declared, 'I am not lost, I am exploring.' She set me thinking about what might be possible if I were to take my interest in speaking seriously. There was curiosity too, as to how my piano might also come into it.

On the final night I went to dinner with several people I knew from the Perth chapter of the association, whom I had met before I left on my camper van trip. They were completely unaware of my story about the piano and the fear. I'd spied a piano in the centre of the hotel bar where we were all staying, and I promised myself that I would play it for them when we got back.

I decided to follow one of the principles suggested from the platform – that sometimes, it's easier to seek forgiveness than to ask permission, so I sat down to play, only to find the lid of the piano locked. My plan foiled, I asked at the desk and was told the piano on the first balcony was unlocked, so I played from there. That suited me just fine, as I couldn't see them and they couldn't see me. In this way, I could pretend that I was just playing for myself.

I was applauded as I sat down, but none of them knew the real scale of the triumph. I felt very proud of myself and found it hard, for a while, to actually concentrate on the conversation.

I wanted it to be normal for me that I could play for others. I didn't want to tell the story of how and why it was such an achievement every time I played, but before I went to bed, I was bursting to tell someone!

On my way to the lift I spotted a guy I had sat next to in one of the sessions. He was talking to one of the main keynote presenters from the USA. Undaunted by that, I ran over and told them my story and how I had just successfully sat down to play for people without them knowing about the fear.

Max Dixon, the American speaker, beamed at me. "Let's go back upstairs and play some more," he said.

Max is a trained actor who brings his knowledge and skills of theatre performance to the speaking fraternity. He is also a composer and has written tunes for Broadway. I had my own personal performance of these after I had played my tunes. Max stands well over six feet tall, and has the widest range of facial expressions I have ever known. His huge hands were able to effortlessly cover the keys, reaching an octave (across eight notes), and beyond, as though it was just a couple of notes. I lost a centimetre of span in my right hand as a result of the injury from the car crash, so I was envious of the ease with which he could reach across that many notes.

As we sat there, Max turned to me, "So, Tracy, why are you here? What is it that you want to speak about?" he asked.

I told him that, in my opinion, communication between the different jobs that people do within the optometry industry was poor. I began to explain how so much potential in people was missed because of the fixed view that others had about their inherent abilities. I told him that, having played every role in that field, I wanted to open up people's perception of what might be possible – and speaking at optometry meetings and conferences might be my way of making a difference.

"No, no, not all that stuff," he retorted. "If this was your last dying breath and there was a message that you wanted to get across to me, what would that be…?"

This question threw me and really made me stop and think. As I sat there looking deep inside for the answer, Max played me another tune. As it came to a close, my answer became clear – "SELF BELIEF!" I almost shouted. "Have belief in yourself!"

That night I had a dream. I saw myself on a big stage giving a really motivating presentation about following your passion, conquering fear and believing in yourself. I ended it by sitting down to play the piano. As I woke the next morning, I remembered every word. The presentation *Live your dream, don't dream your life!* which had begun as a ten minute presentation for a speech contest (as I mentioned in the introduction) was now much more fully developed, and I could see how I could bring all my experiences together to inspire people to take action beyond their doubts and fears.

I called Max on the hotel's internal phone and related the dream. He said his cheeks were tingling and that this was exactly why he does what he does for a living. We met for breakfast, and he spent four hours coaching me on how to powerfully deliver a story within a presentation.

I am convinced that that chance encounter has saved me years of trying to figure out what my message as a speaker is.

You never know where a conversation might lead you if you are willing to share your passion and mission with others.

I learnt very quickly that it wasn't about the notes I got wrong during a performance; it was more about the love of music that I was able to share and what that evoked for other people as well as for me.

If, like me, you've been brought up with a dog in the family, you'll know how there is an increase in conversation with complete strangers that happens when you have a dog with you. Play a piano in public and someone will come over to talk to you in much the same way – try it!

What's the Piano in Your Life?
Having seen the difference that speaking up has made with regard to leading me to resources and people, I want you to think about how you might use this avenue of potential for yourself. Make it a game – see how many times you can bring your story and current challenge into a conversation with people.

Remember also the value of being a connector for other people. Know the questions to ask that will help you make a connection for someone in their own quest for progress.

What Goes Around Comes Around!

Notice what links are provided as you use and polish these skills. Watch out for the opportunity to reach for a higher goal as challenges come your way.

Who could you talk to about what it is that you want to achieve?

Remember:
Not having a piano is not a water-tight reason for not being able to play!

Summary
- Be a 'connector' for other people.
- Speak up and talk about your quest or desire.

- Let others know why your goal is important to you and what they can do to help.
- Identify what you stand to gain by taking action.
- Use positive language – in your thoughts and spoken words.
- Take action.
- Keep the momentum going.

3 Get Some Help!

There is no such thing as a self-made man. You will reach your goals only with the help of others.

George Shinn

Investing in a piano and going back to lessons were essential steps en route to my goal. Figuring out who could help me also played a vital part. I got really serious about both of these aspects once I was back in the UK, and my campervan tour of Australia had come to an end. That help was found in many different places and from many different people.

All too often though, when we have a goal that is outside the realms of work, and that is not 'professional', we do not take it as seriously as we would if it were a work goal. Somehow we believe that we should be able to arrive at our intended destination without help from other people. We don't always consider it worthy of financial investment or a structured plan of action. As I had found in the past, this attitude can prevent us from moving forward as quickly as we might and is likely to cause frustration in the process.

By getting some help and investing time and money towards your goal, you are making a commitment and are more likely to reach your objective with the least amount of stress.

Consider the following four things when you think about the help and support you may need to arrive at your goal:

- WHAT do you need?

- WHO can help you?

- WHERE can you find them?

- HOW can you help yourself?

WHAT Do You Need?

There is a massive difference between learning to play a piece of music for pleasure at home and learning to play it for a performance before an audience. The level of attention to detail and the foundation of skill have to be much stronger. Your expertise must hold up under the extra pressure of an attentive audience. The same is true for giving speeches.

In order to play in a concert or present before an audience, you have to know your material inside out, 'note perfect' with your eyes shut, without losing concentration while someone tries to interrupt you by banging on the door. Or at least, that's how it feels.

So to determine what you need for your quest, consider the following:

- What is your skill level now?

- What is the outcome you desire?

- Under what circumstances do you intend to perform?

Begin with the end in mind – if you have your sights firmly set, you can look objectively at where you are and where you want to be. Ask yourself—

How **B I G** is the gap?

Knowing your objective and having a time line for its completion creates a clear vision of what needs to happen in between. The next step is to think about what you need to do and how much help and support you will need from others, in order to get there.

Understand WHY You Want 'It'
Identifying why you want to achieve this goal is perhaps the single most motivating force in the exercise. Once you know this, you'll have the necessary emotional commitment to support you.

My reason 'why' came about through a life-threatening event and from almost leaving it too late. The car crash and the reality of a broken hand that might never have been fit enough to use provided the impetus to make a change. Almost losing the opportunity to ever play again was my wake-up call and brought home for me the importance in my life of playing a piano. I was no longer willing to let fear and procrastination get in the way of putting a once-treasured passion back into my life.

Get Beyond the 'Excuses'
I used to be as guilty as many others for letting 'reasons' (otherwise known as excuses – although I didn't recognise them under this name at the time) get in the way of what I wanted to achieve. If you can clearly identify what those reasons are, you are in a much stronger position to tackle them one by one, and to create a plan of how to get around, beyond or through them. With a bit of creative thinking and input from other people, it will be possible to find a way.

> *If you want something done you'll find a way. If you don't want something done you'll find an excuse.*
>
> Donald Trump

If now is not the right time for you to chase your passion, know that it doesn't have to stay on the shelf gathering dust forever. There are things that you can do in the meantime to keep the idea alive, like talking about it or having a symbol that represents it. Creating an album full of pictures of the things that you would like to have in your life one day, is a great way to do this. The more often that you take a look, the more likely that without you even realising, your subconscious mind will be coming up with a plan to make it a reality.

Keeping a special place for those thoughts and aspirations prevents them from becoming buried and forgotten. You never know when you might come across someone who could help to turn that dream into reality before you thought possible.

Frustrations in each of our lives will be found in different areas. The following examples are meant to stimulate your thoughts and help you to think of a few ways around your own roadblocks.

Investment of Time and Money

Investment of money can sometimes be hard to justify in our minds. If you feel you don't have enough money to achieve your goal right now, could you find people, friends, or associates who may be able to help you without the need for money to change hands?

Do you have a skill that you could swap in return for their help?

Remember, not having a piano didn't stop me from learning to play one.

Where there's a will there's a way!

I am often reluctant to invest in a massage, considering it a non-essential expense. However, when I don't have a massage for a long time, my neck and shoulders get tense from the repetitive movements involved in my work, from driving and from sitting in front of a computer. When I finally do give in and go, it is a real relief and leaves me with more freedom of movement and energy to perform more efficiently in other areas of my life. I always wonder why I left it so long and realise what a difference it would provide to my sense of wellbeing if I could make plans to incorporate it on a regular basis. It's a bit like regular maintenance of your car. It, like you, will run much more effectively if regularly taken care of, rather than managing maintenance only when a crisis comes along. (I'm working on it … having written this, I remind myself yet again. I will book a massage tomorrow!)

How often does your car stay dirty because you don't have time to wash it yourself? Every time you get in it, you are left feeling frustrated until finally, there comes a point when a willing volunteer knocks on the door. You hand them the £5 requested to clean it, and the next time you get in the car, you instantly feel better. Just consider how much of a drain this frustration has seeped away in the mean time. If you had planned a regular clean and had immediately taken some action when you were not happy, all that energy could have been focused in a more positive direction.

If your reason for not doing something is a question of time, think again! If you are open to suggestion and willing to think laterally, you will find, as I did, that there is often a way to get around the problem.

Lack of time is not always the major roadblock that it may initially seem. I'm sure you could manage to claw back a few minutes or hours here and there by delegating some household or administrative tasks. My friend Clare is an inspiration to me. For as long as I have known her she has insisted that having a cleaner for four hours a week could be justified. Clare believes that, since she can earn more per hour than she pays the cleaner, even if she has very little work, her first priority is the cleaner.

Are there other areas in your life where you could cut back to make time for something you really want to do?

What household chores could you farm out to allow you more time and more energy to do what you really want to do?

Could you, like Clare, pay someone else to do your housework?

Could you shop online? Ask your children to go to the post office for you? Clare pays her 12- and 14-year-old to photocopy and collate her training material and copy the CDs she gives to students.

What Could You Do?

Similarly, investing in regular, planned support from others to help you reach your goal will ensure you reach it with greater speed, efficiency and a positive sense of wellbeing. H ving this regular input will also provide a constant flow of encouragement, which will offer support and inject a regular boost to your belief so that you can achieve your goal.

Other things to consider that will help you to make the most effective use of your time are:

- The time of day you plan to work on things

- Knowing how to avoid distractions

(More about this follows in Chapter 7, Practise, Practise, Practise)

There are many different methods by which we can learn, whether from a book, an expert or teacher, or in a classroom situation. Knowing which methods suit our personality and honouring that will save time and spare the feelings of frustration. Time invested in making progress will leave you with more energy and vigour for the rest of your life, so it may actually add more time than you realise. If I were to try to improve my practical piano skills by just reading a book, I know that I would soon lose my interest and determination – and it would only increase my theoretical knowledge, not my practical ability.

If I have a piano lesson booked, my commitment to practise increases dramatically. The reasons for not playing don't disappear; it's just that the importance of putting aside time to learn is more at the front of my mind, and so I make time to do it. Thus my practical ability improves AND it provides motivation to take action.

Invest in yourself – you are worth it and it will pay dividends!

Accept Your Starting Point

Accept your current abilities and plan how you are going to reach the new desired level of knowledge or skill. Once you have your plan in place, resist the temptation to beat yourself up mentally for not being further along the path.

Acknowledge that if it's a higher goal than you've reached for in the past, repeating what you have done before isn't enough to get you to where you want to go.

Initially, when I started again with the piano lessons, I could so easily have felt frustrated, comparing the memory of how I used to be able to play, compared to my current ability that had16 years worth of rust to remove and fingers that couldn't move as fast or as far as they could before the damage to my hand. I had to accept my skill level exactly where it was, be aware of the deep-rooted desire I had to change it, and be proud that I was taking action to do so. Bearing in mind that I was really lucky to be alive and have any chance of playing again at all was a useful thought to keep things in perspective.

I have a friend who is always keen to hear about what I have been up to with playing the piano and performing. Like me, she passed most of her piano exams as a youngster. Every time I visit her home, the keyboard comes out and we both play. She tells me how she would love to be able to play again properly and I sense the envy – we recognise so well that which we have felt ourselves! I see in my friend's eyes the frustration and disappointment at where her talents lie now having left them dormant for so long – but I also recognise the great desire for it not to be that way. I encourage her to go back to lessons and she says, 'I can't go back yet, and have the teacher go over old ground – I need to practise before I go.' Of course, the practice never will happen while there is no one waiting to hear her progress each week. I know this from years of feeling exactly that way myself.

As we grow older and our responsibilities increase, it is all too easy for our passion and interests to be considered insignificant and pushed aside by our roles of partner and parent. Time and money can always be spent elsewhere, and a passion for music, or whatever your passion is, is rarely considered a priority.

I would question the validity of such an ultimate sacrifice. We want our children to live a fulfilled and passionate life, yet we live a life in denial of our own needs and often neglect to include aspects that could add to our own sense of fulfilment. Who has made the biggest impression on you – someone who leads by words or by example?

WHO can help you?

- Experts
- Coaches
- Friends
- Role models

- People following a similar quest

- Those who have already 'done it'

- People who challenge you

- People who inspire you

- People who nurture you

And the ones to watch out for –

- Cynics

A wise man will make more opportunities than he finds.

Sir Francis Bacon

Seeking the help of a supportive network of people will help you uncover far greater potential, and help you reach greater heights than you could achieve alone. It's like the difference between sitting on a see-saw and hoping to create the momentum yourself, compared to having a willing friend providing weight and support at the other end.

Share Your Success

There is much joy to be found in sharing your road to achievement. There's a whole army of people out there who you might enlist for help if you are willing to look and know where to start your search. Giving people a role to play and letting them know specifically how they can help you achieve your goal can be a massive help as you pursue your goal. By planning your team before you begin, you will pave the way to speedy progress.

How Could You Make Use of The Following?

Experts

Choose your teacher with care. If you are inspired by who they are and what they do with their life, then your aspirations, commitment and rate of progress will increase in direct proportion to that. Learn from someone you admire.

Deciding to go back to lessons for me began with a visit to Mrs Hind, my music teacher from primary school. She was flattered that I had come back to ask her for tuition, but said that she was teaching her grandchildren and not taking on other students anymore, and enjoying her retirement. Nevertheless, she was delighted I was making use of my ability. So I dug out the Yellow Pages and, after a few conversations with different teachers, I opted for Liz Paling, a Scottish lady who had just moved down to the Midlands to teach at Loughborough College. What I liked about her was that she performed in a quartet and played solos for weddings and that she had taken the plunge to move from Scotland to be nearer to her father. She suggested that we meet to see if we could work together. I met her at the Music Department at Loughborough College. The place had a fantastic buzz about it. Mixing with the full-time students inspired me and added fuel to the already burning desire to learn.

Coaches

Sportsmen and women use coaches all the time. In fact, many of the best athletes employ two or three of them. Today, executive and life coaching is hugely popular. Rather than tell you what to do, a coach helps you to explore your own potential and encourages you to believe in yourself and succeed. A tennis player may have one coach for motivation and attitude, another for strategy and another for skill. Each has their own specialism.

I have had help and support from many different coaches over the years I have been pursuing self-development. They all helped me to keep on track with the plan that I had created to achieve my goal. The value was as much in having someone that knew what I had committed to do, and by when, as it was to have someone to talk to about it. They have been invaluable in keeping me focused not only on producing this book, so that my experiences can help other people, but in encouraging me to take the same bold action in all areas of my life.

Working with a coach usually spans a 3-4 month period if you want to see effective change, but the arrangement can last as for as long or as short a time as you like. Some coaches work face-to-face, but most sessions usually take place via the phone with back up by email.

Curly Martin, author of *The Life Coaching Handbook*, compares coaching to motorway maintenance and construction.

'It fills and removes the ruts of life to build a smooth surface … to take you to the destinations you really want to visit, rather than remain in the slow lane of inactivity, drifting without purpose or direction', she writes.

There's plenty of information on the Internet to help you find a coach. Choose someone who inspires you. Many coaches charge £50, £60 or more per hour. Executive coaches can charge up to five times that! But please don't let money be a reason for not making use of this option. There are new coaches out there who are training and would jump at the chance to make a difference en route to your, and their, success. Contact any of the institutions that teach coaching to ask if they have students who are in need of this option. Or put an advert on a networking site like Ecademy or Linked-in to help you find them.

Be aware that anyone can call themselves a 'life coach'. There are organisations who offer formal training and certification which vary in length and intensity. In my experience, the best coaches aren't always the ones with the relevant piece of paper.

I had purpose and direction by the bucket-load before I found my coach, but having a coach was one more piece of infrastructure to keep my plan on track, making sure that other areas of my life moved forward too.

Friends

People who care about you, encourage you and ask after your progress are invaluable. They help you to feel supported and have a knack of putting life's little challenges into perspective. Your friends may also have skills to help you in your quest.

Many people I have met through the Professional Speakers Association who have become friends have filled this role for me, sharing knowledge that has helped on a personal as well as performance level.

Playing piano duets with my friend Becky reminded me how to have fun and widened my vision beyond the drill of day-to-day practice.

What or who could you include in your life that might create the same level of support for you?

Role Models and Mentors

No doubt there are people whom you admire. What specific qualities do they have that cause you to feel this way about them?

As you find more and more of the people in these categories, identify the personal attributes that allow them to be successful and an expert in their area. Is that prominent quality, for example, tenacity, patience, or persistence? By practising some of these attributes yourself, you will find your success rate expands. Regular contact with such people will provide you with a dose of inspiration and encourage you to step up to a higher level of achievement under that positive influence.

People Following a Similar Quest

Being amongst like-minded people will always spark your passion and give you the confidence to take bold steps. Just being around other people who are pushing their boundaries and expanding their lives can help you think outside the box and encourage you to keep taking bold action steps yourself. My fellow speakers amongst the PSA, the students at Loughborough College, and my colleagues from the self-development courses I attended provided this support for me.

Look For Those Who Have Already 'Done It'

One of the memories I held in my mind when dealing with my own fear was of a TV documentary led by the journalist, Martin Bashir. I was in my early teens at the time and remember being glued to the set. In his role as a psychotherapist, Martin was coaching a professional female guitarist who had lost her nerve to perform, although, she had played to capacity audiences at the Albert Hall in London when she was younger. I don't recall what happened to create this anxiety, but I was fascinated about how they were going to cure it.

Over a six-week period she received coaching in specific methods to enable her to conquer that fear. One method included getting her to practise at home with her favourite rug beneath her feet. The rug represented a secure area in which she could feel at peace and not be disturbed by outside thoughts or views from other people. After she became used to this feeling of security, she was encouraged to go to the venue and, again, play with the rug beneath her, bringing with her the feelings of security and peace from her practice at home. As the concert drew closer she played at the venue but without the rug, nevertheless still visualising it to be there, reminding herself of that secure feeling. Practising these techniques allowed her to feel confident as she again performed before a large audience.

Knowing that someone else had felt that fear and had found a method to deal with it, on a much grander scale than anything I intended, reinforced my belief that I could also learn how to quash the fear.

People Who Challenge You

Mix with people who see your potential and dare you to rise to their level of belief in you. They will be very useful allies in your quest. You will stand taller and jump higher in your desire to preserve their faith in you.

All of the opportunities that I had to play in concerts were as a direct result of talking to other people about what I was up to. Although the performances were nerve-wracking at the time, it was those very events that gave me major milestones to help me reach the big goal that I talk about in the next chapter. Accepting challenges and recommendations suggested by other people can really increase your length of stride and level of progress.

Make sure though that these challenges are in line with your goal. If they aren't, then they may provide an opportunity for you to be sidetracked. We are all good at displacement activities that take us away from our goals. I know from my own past experience that my bathroom was always at its cleanest when I was supposed to be studying for exams!

Seek Those Who Inspire You

My teachers and my friends were a constant source of inspiration. I also found myself spurred on by watching other talented musicians at work. Of course, it can work the other way, too. When I went to see a group of young Russian piano prodigies in action, whose ages ranged from 8 – 14, my resolve wavered between feeling completely inspired and the thought that I should 'quit now'. Seeing how adept they were at such a young age brought back a childlike feeling of, 'I'll never be good enough so why bother?' followed immediately by, 'WOW! It's so great to be able to play a piano!'

When you are inspired by people who are so much better or more experienced than you, keep it in perspective and use the experience as a positive tool to aid your progress. Choose your reaction!

Sometimes when the going gets a bit tough, helping someone else along the way can put a spring back in your own step and relight a spark to get you back on track.

Those Who Nurture You

It's important to recognise those people who look out for your welfare. My mum can be guaranteed to tell me that I have done enough work and it's time to take a break. In my younger and more cynical days, I would sometimes view this as a lack of encouragement. Having gained wisdom with age, I am much more appreciative and can see those comments for what they are – born out love and caring. These days, I take the time to listen…well, most of the time!

If the rest of your life falls apart because of your quest and desire to achieve, it will be a hollow victory in the end when you have no one left to celebrate it with, so just be aware of those who love and support you in ways that may not always be instantly obvious.

And the ones to watch out for...

Cynics

You may find yourself dealing with people around you who doubt your ability to achieve your goal and question its validity. Beware of those who drain your energy and determination. Quit talking to them about your intentions and avoid letting them in on the act. When this is a partner or family member it can be really tricky, but standing up to this and moving forward regardless will do an enormous amount of good for your self-confidence in that relationship. Allow the cynicism to strengthen your resolve. Make a specific request of the person in terms of what they could do to make a positive difference for you. If their answer is not supportive, then take a look in the resource section of this book for other texts that may be of use.

WHERE Will You Find Them?

To create your Support Team look to your friends and family, to experts you might find on the Internet or from the Yellow Pages or by referral. Look for links in the books that you read, relevant articles in the press, or check your local notice board at the library or in the supermarket.

When you are on the lookout for information and resources, it is amazing how much more you will find. Many of the suggestions about where to find these people will come from talking to others about your challenge.

I was in London one weekend in the lead-up to the second concert I was to play in. I wanted somewhere to rehearse so that my practice schedule would not be interrupted, even though I was away from home. I came across a piano shop and thought I would ask if I could sit in the corner and play for a while. The 'Closed' sign on the door didn't deter me, as I could see someone playing at the back of the shop. The lady who came to the door listened to my story and invited me in. She introduced herself as Maria Yugina. She was there waiting for a piano student of her own and so practice for me wasn't an option, but she was interested to hear more about the concert and what I was going to play in it.

She told me that she had studied at the Moscow College of Music for many years and was in London to improve her English. I was intrigued and asked if she had time to play something for me. The performance I witnessed was amazing, and I stood wide-eyed in awe. The thing that made the greatest impact on me was that she had such small hands compared to me, and yet was able to stretch them so far. I mentioned earlier that as a result of the car crash, the span of my right hand was now smaller. I thought until that point that I just had to accept it. Watching her play blew that 'reason' right out of the water.

When Maria finished she asked me to play for her. As I sat down and looked at the keys, my mind went blank; I couldn't even remember the first notes of the piece I was due to perform at the concert in a few short weeks. She smiled and asked me to play something that I loved. I played *Robin's Return*, a tune that my very first piano teacher, Mrs Hind, used to play at the end of my lessons.

With words of praise and encouragement, Maria showed me how to open the piece in grander and more striking way. Her method involved pressing into the keys with quite a lot of force, and then lifting the hands off with the sustain pedal pressed down to carry the sound. The technique was not something that I had ever been taught in quite that way before. She went on to show me much more too, and by the time we finished, I felt like I had just sat a three-hour exam. My concentration had been 110% as I soaked up like a sponge all that she was willing to share with me.

It was the most intriguing and fascinating lesson I had ever had. I tried at the end of the lesson to go back to my original piece of music, but the block on the notes was still there. Her advice to me was that I shouldn't be playing a piece in a concert if I couldn't remember the first notes. It was incredibly frustrating.

Over the next few months, I made a point of travelling to London for more lessons with Maria. Under her guidance I couldn't help but wonder how far I could take my ability. Maria, being a performer at heart, was eager to become a part of the concert I was preparing for. When she first asked, I was very unsure about appearing on the same platform, but she assured me that it would be good for both of us, and she offered to provide the finale if the organisers so wished. Knowing that we would eventually both be sharing a platform gave that much more focus to the lessons.

Finding Maria was like finding a golden nugget and made a big difference, but it wasn't in the most obvious place – if I hadn't been open to opportunities I might have missed out. My lessons still continued with my regular teacher, but there is more than one person out there who can help you arrive at your destination. The broader the input, the richer the result. Keep an open mind, because there are possibilities everywhere to find people who might help you.

HOW Can You Help Yourself?
By becoming an expert in your subject you will be much better informed, knowledgeable and able to help yourself as well as receiving help from others.

Books

I've read so many self-help books that I have them sprawling off the shelves in my house. You can find a list of the ones I found most useful in the Resources section at the end of this book.

I am one of those people who love to write in books. Take a peek into one of mine and you will see it covered in highlighter pen and red and blue biro. If that is not your style, and you like to leave books pristine, maybe you could use Post-it® Notes and put them in the relevant pages with a few comments jotted down.

I make notes so that I can go back to the book again and again to remind myself of the salient points. Some I return to frequently, finding different learning points useful as life's circumstances change. The ones that made the biggest impact when I was working toward the concerts were:

Feel the Fear and Do It Anyway by Susan Jeffers

What I remember most – the affirmation, 'I know I can do it!'

and

How to Stop Worrying and Start Living by Dale Carnegie

The part I have most often read at 3am with a concert looming, is this advice:

- 'Think in day tight compartments' meaning, do what you can with the day in front of you. Don't concern yourself with what comes next, focus more on 'now.'

- 'Gather all the information'. Often by finding out more information, we are more confidently able to make our choices and take the next step forward.

While I have been in the process of writing this book, I have come across two books that I wish I had read before the s:

mer Game of Music by Barry Green and Tim Gallwey

aī d

The New Psycho-Cybernetics by Maxwell Maltz

The Inner Game of Music has great exercises to help you focus on producing the best performance. *The New Psycho-Cybernetics* is great for getting you to question your limiting thoughts about what you are capable of.

If you are not sure where to start, ask the people in your Support Team to recommend some books for you.

Just reading a book did not make a difference to my life. It was only by putting the knowledge and suggestions into practice and continually pushing my comfort zone that I was able to see my ability grow.

How are you doing so far with what you have read here? Be willing to put it to the test and know that I am eager to hear the results!

Internet
There is a vast wealth of knowledge available on the Internet, but beware of being sidetracked into other topics and spending more time than intended without the required result. The Internet is a great way of finding other people who are out there doing a similar thing. Have a look at the business networking sites like Ecademy (which I mentioned earlier), also Magenta Circle, and Linked-In. There are quite a few out there. People listed on these sites comment on interests outside, as well as inside, work. They mention upcoming social and business events so there is an opportunity to create friendships as well as business colleagues. Website addresses and contact details

are in the Resources section.

Press Articles

I have an army of people who tell me about articles and even send me things that I might be interested in because they know what I am up to. By sharing your passion with other people, you could tap into a wealth of other resources just because they are on the lookout for you too. Don't forget to make this a two way street!

Organisations and Clubs

There are all sort of Professional or business clubs which can provide a rich source of support, advice and information. Oddly, the best advice can turn up in some unlikely places.

I recommend that you take a look at local networking groups, special interest groups, professional associations, and breakfast clubs that specialise in your field. You will find a list of those I particularly like or have had recommended to me in the Resources section.

What's the Piano in Your Life?

When you consider how much potential help is out there, your goal can feel that much more easily achievable. You don't need to re-invent the wheel. There are plenty of people available who know the methods that work. Be willing to seek help from those who can make a difference. Going it alone can be a very tiresome, lonely and frustrating place.

Fill in the chart below to see what you have at your disposal and to highlight where you could look for some help. (A copy of this can be downloaded from my web site if you don't want to write in the book; visit www.tracyplaice.com)

WHO can help?	WHERE will I look for them?	Name	HOW specifically can they help me?	Qualities that they have that I can aspire to
Teachers				
Experts				
Role models				
Challengers				
Nurturers				
Inspiration sources				
Done it before				
Supportive Friends				

What resources are you going to use to become your own expert in this field?

1

2

3

4

5

Summary

- Understand the gap between where you are compared with where you want to be.
- Know your reason for wanting to achieve your goal.
- Get some help.
- Build a Support Team.
- Make yourself an expert.

4 | Set a Goal That Inspires You

Whatever the mind can conceive and believe, it can achieve.
Napoleon Hill

What really started a concerted and very focused period of action was having a clear-cut, inspiring goal to aim for. My original intention of conquering my fear of playing a piano in public had no real specific criteria to meet, or any deadline or event by which I would know that I had achieved it. I was thrown a challenge by someone at a conference, which gave me a clearly defined target, and did have a deadline. The opportunity to reach for this particular goal was set for me by Steve McDermott, an inspiring motivational speaker who you will hear about below.

Sometimes it takes another person, who is not subject to our inner voices of doubt, to see the real potential and challenge us to even greater heights. Accepting this higher challenge requires that we take on board another person's level of belief in us, rather than listening to our own often limiting sense of self. It is only by speaking up about what you want to achieve that these people who will challenge you can appear.

Setting goals will give you definite posts to aim for and a time frame. By accepting challenges from other people, I have achieved so much more than I set out to do, and so much more than just being able to confidently play a piano in public.

Nothing gives you more satisfaction in life than to know that you are on the road to success and achievement. And nothing stands as a bigger challenge than making the most of yourself.

The Magic ofThinking Big by David Schwartz

I was about to discover a broader set of skills and a deeper awareness of what it took to achieve my goal.

The Challenge

Once I was back in the UK with my trip around Australia having come to an end, I was eager to continue my links with the professional speaking community. I had researched information about the UK version of the National Speakers Association and found their affiliate organisation called the Professional Speakers Association. I had only been back a couple of months when I went to their annual convention.

The result of one chance conversation over dinner, and another whilst I was greeting a friend at the bar, raised 'the bar' for me and set the scene for the level of action I needed to take over a whole year.

Dinner at the convention on the Saturday night was 'safari style', meaning that after every course we all moved to different tables. The idea was to meet as many people as possible.

For the third course I sat next to Steve Head, who introduced himself as a high performance coach. As we chatted, I told him about my goal of conquering my fear of playing a piano in public and asked for his advice. Over the next hour, our heads were bent over a napkin on the table on which he presented his theories and strategies for high achievement. We must have talked for over an hour, completely oblivious to what was going on around us.

As we parted company to chat to other people, I felt empowered and confident from the knowledge Steve had shared, coupled with his offer to help me. I walked over to the bar to say hello to Trish Tucker, an Australian speaker I had met earlier that day.

Before she had a chance to introduce me to the people around her, a man I didn't know said, "That conversation at the table over there – it looked really interesting – what was that was all about?" He added, "I'm Steve McDermott, by the way".

I told him my story about not playing a piano for sixteen years, about the fear that had stopped me sharing my passion for music, and my determination to conquer it in view of the car crash, my broken hand and the prospect that I might never have been able to play again.

"That's interesting," he replied, "I've just been invited to give the opening keynote at next year's conference and I'm going to talk about beliefs and how you can change them. How about you play the piano to introduce me; I give my speech with some examples – then you're my live example. I'll tell them your story, how you conquered your fear, and get you back on stage at the end to play again. What d'you think?"

"OK," I said, before my brain had engaged to consider the consequences.

The prospect took my breath away, and I was a little stunned as I smiled back at him. The conversation continued, but a little voice somewhere in the region of my stomach was screaming, 'NO! She really means, NO!!'

When there was a lull in the conversation, I went back to where Steve Head was sitting. "You'll never guess what just happened at the bar," I said. "I've just been invited by Steve McDermott to play the piano to introduce him when he opens the convention next year. He wants me to be the live example in his presentation about beliefs and how you can change them. I said, 'Yes!'."

"That's great!" His enthusiasm lit up his eyes. "But, if you're going to perform in front of 200 international speakers in year's time, how many times do you think you've got to perform in public for that to be easy?"

"I don't know," I replied. "Twenty?"

"Ok, so when are you going to get started?"

The gap between where my skills and confidence were at that point, and where they needed to be in a year's time, was huge.

Begin with the end in mind.

Brian Tracy

There was no set plan in the early days – I just did everything that I could think of and more. I made a vow to myself to play the piano whenever and wherever I saw one. All my friends, family and colleagues knew this. Telling them was my way of ensuring that I couldn't back out of it, especially if I came across a situation that I might have thought 'too difficult' or 'inconvenient'.

Continued Self-Development and More Challenges

When I returned to the UK I still wanted to continue on my course of self-development and signed up for a year long programme aimed at developing skills in the area of team leadership and management. Our personal objectives were to work towards achieving a new goal every four months. Monthly team meetings were held in London. There were about fifty of us on the course, but locally we would meet in a group of eight and be supported by a personal coach and someone who had completed the training before.

This training was actually run all over Europe, and every four months we would visit another European destination to meet with people following the same course from Israel, Holland, France and Germany. This meant that we were challenged to think globally about our projects right from the start. The international weekends put us among 300 or so people who were all doing amazing things. As we heard their stories and what had to be overcome to achieve their objectives, stepping boldly outside the comfort zone became more like 'normal' behaviour because everyone was doing it.

My first goal concentrated on the musical performances that I wanted to add to my track record. Talking about this within the group unveiled many other people who also had musical talent. Some of them had that aspect firmly in their current lives, but many, like me, had let it lie dormant for a long time. However, they were willing to dust off their skills in pursuit of fun and progress.

One of my fellow participants – Odyle, took the lead and organised a concert for us all to perform in. There were a couple of professional musicians on the course, so this was to be a musical extravaganza, stretching from amateur to professional performers, with every level in between. We had two months to sell the tickets and polish our skills. The event was to be held in a grand old concert hall in Shepherd's Bush.

Meanwhile, I had returned to work as an Optician. Locum work through agencies allowed me to have the flexibility I needed to attend the course in London and take time out to further my education in the speaking arena.

A Deadline Sooner Than Expected

Sometimes the challenges set for you by others can appear overwhelming, and your inner critic may tell you that you're not ready yet. Your thoughts and feelings about how you would feel if you did say 'yes' and what impact that might have on your level of action and commitment, can help you to decide whether or not to jump right in and go for it.

To go back to my story of the self-development course – we were encouraged to keep in touch with people who had already completed the course. The purpose of this was to offer inspiration to them as they heard stories about what the members of the 'team' were up to, and also to allow them to take on a mentor role to help guide us when the going got tough.

I'd been put in touch with a chap called Duncan who lived near me in the Midlands. He had completed this course a couple of years earlier. Chatting to him on the phone, I relayed the story of my piano challenge from Steve McDermott and told him about the concert that was planned in Shepherd's Bush. Putting my 'bold hat' on, I asked if he would like to hear the piece I was going to perform. He agreed, and so I set the phone to loudspeaker and sat at the piano to play *Maple Leaf Rag*.

I had been practising my music and listening back to it using the 'record' button on my piano. This was the next level up as far as exposing my talents to public ears was concerned. It made me hot under the collar, but I felt proud of myself for being willing to continue to step outside my comfort zone.

Duncan applauded my performance and then said, "As a bit of a hobby, I organise Old Time Music Hall events in Sheffield every six months. The next one is on 5th May, in a few weeks time; would you like to play in it?"

As I checked my diary, endless limitations popped into my head:

- It's even sooner than the first concert I am going to perform in.
- I'm away in Skegness doing locum work as an Optician the week before.
- Where will I practise?
- I'm in Wetherby at a Professional Speakers Association meeting the morning of the concert.
- There'll be lots of travel.
- I'll be too tired.

But then I thought about how I would feel on the Sunday if I'd played in the concert on that Saturday night. I knew that I would feel amazing if I did it – and would never forgive myself if I didn't.

I thought about the level of commitment I would have to maintain to practise. If I knew I was going to be playing in the concert, it would ensure I had no excuse for not practising even while I was away.

I had already proved to myself in Melbourne that it didn't matter if I didn't have my own piano; it was not a valid reason not to be able to play. I asked myself how many people I would have to share my quest with daily to be able to get what

I wanted in the form of a piano to practise on while I worked away in Skegness.

I took the plunge and accepted the challenge!

The Power Of A Deadline

It is amazing how resourceful you can become when you have a deadline looming!

A few weeks before I went to Skegness, I called the Tourist Information Office to sort out accommodation and explain my challenge. I told them why I was doing it and asked for their help in finding somewhere to stay and to practise the piano. It was not a request that they had had before, but they were very happy to try to help.

They only knew of one hotel with a piano, and when I rang to book, I was disappointed to hear that they were due to be closed that week. The lady at the Tourist Information Office kindly got out the local Yellow Pages to look for music shops, only to find there wasn't one close by. So I asked about music teachers and rang them. None that I called were able to help me, as they had teaching commitments, but one of them suggested I call the local schools. Another of the reception-ists I spoke to at a hotel suggested I try the local theatre. Unfortunately, they had a play on that week and I was told that I wouldn't be able to get to the piano, as it was due to be 'shoved into the back corner'.

I had already made it known to the Optician practice manager what I was looking for and all of his staff had been asked, but no resources had been found. When I arrived at my B&B in Skegness, I still had no firm plans about where or how I was going to lay my hands on a piano. This did not daunt or disappoint me, as I had faith that I would make it happen if I was willing to speak to enough people about what I needed.

Some of you who don't play an instrument will probably be thinking, 'If you had practised enough, surely it wouldn't be that important to play right up until the concert?'

Those of you who do play will know what I mean when I say that daily reinforcement is crucial when you have such an important event looming. Without daily practice your fingers are not as nimble and do not always do as you think you have asked them to! Also, from the point of view of keeping my mind quiet and my nerves at bay, the more practice I could do before the event, the less would be the churning of my mind and stomach before and also at the event. This was the very first time I was to perform on a stage with a fee-paying audience – I was determined to do everything in my power to be ready.

On my first day at work in Skegness, I stood outside the shop in the rain waiting for the practice to open. The first patient was also there with his mother, huddled underneath an umbrella. I chatted to them and brought hobbies and pianos into the conversation. It turned out the young boy was learning to play the keyboard. They gave me the telephone number of his teacher, and that night and the next, I played at her house after work.

It was difficult, as her piano was in her lounge and she sat in her armchair behind me while I played, but I had to get over the discomfort because my deadline was looming. The plus side was that she kindly made no charge. I was very grateful for her hospitality.

The piano teacher had also been able to recommend a school where I might be able to practise. Two mornings later that week, I impressed even myself, as I went there to rehearse at 7.30 am before going to work!

It was a good spot to practise as the pupils were arriving in dribs and drabs. I had to choose not to give in to the embarrassment that I felt about them listening to me. The music teacher who I had organised this with also came to introduce himself. Playing the piece straight through for him was a good test for me and exposed me to the feelings that I was going to have to face full on in a few days time, with a whole auditorium of people listening.

One night when I didn't have a venue in which to rehearse, ever the optimist, I decided to take a drive and look for somewhere to play. I came across a village hall with a few cars parked outside and went to investigate. There was a piano in the corner, but a group of people sat around the edge of the room about to take a dance class. Undeterred, I drove on and came across a Butlin's style holiday camp. I drove in and went to talk to the security guard. I told him about my quest and the looming concert. I asked if there was anywhere that I might be able to play a piano on site.

He went to get the duty manager, and I repeated my story for him. The manager smiled at me and said there was karaoke going on in the main bar, but that the stage next door wasn't being used and had a piano. He showed me through to a large theatre, he flicked on all the house lights and we climbed the stairs onto the stage. There in the wings was a grand piano. He said it was all mine for as long as I wanted.

It was actually the best practice session I had had all week, as I had to concentrate so hard to ignore the noise blaring away from the karaoke next door. Because of the noise it also meant I had to play loud to hear myself above the din, so I just let go and had some fun. With great bravado I pretended to be a cross between Bobby Crush and Liberace. It's amazing how much confidence I had when I knew there was no danger of being heard!

I felt an amazing sense of satisfaction as I left the venue that night – proud that, even in a town where I knew no one, because I had a deadline to meet, I had really pushed the boat out to meet my objective to find somewhere to play.

Unexpected Results

Talking to people about what I wanted to achieve became and still is a way of life. Because so many people knew what I was doing, the support I received was fantastic.

When you are on course towards your goal, your passion becomes infectious. People start to have faith in you, and they believe that you know what you are talking about. Once you are on track you can get some amazing, unexpected opportunities and results.

Here are a couple of mine …

After Dinner Entertainment

At one of the Professional Speakers' meetings in the UK, I met a lady called Mo Shapiro. As well as being an author, inspirational speaker and broadcaster, she loves to impersonate Victoria Wood. When she heard about my quest with the piano, she said, "I can't play the piano; would you consider accompanying me when I sing Victoria Wood's songs?"

Learning to play to accompany someone singing was a whole new ball game. The first practice session we had together was in a piano shop near her house. I was used to finding places to play by then! I had learnt the first verse and the chorus and could play it quite well at home. But when I tried to play as she sang along, my ability plummeted – distracted by her singing. It was so bad (my playing not her singing!) that I had to resort to playing the tune with one hand and one note at a time.

I felt useless and was sure that she would turn to me and at any minute say, 'Well, it was a nice idea but I don't think it will work'. I am so grateful that she was able to see beyond my stumbling preliminary efforts. It marked the beginning of a really supportive friendship both personally and professionally for me.

The piece of music we were to perform changed key six times. That meant that even though I had learnt the first verse, when those notes were played each time the next verse came along, it would be different notes I would be playing. I found learning the piece really hard. It was extremely confusing to commit it to memory. Sheer bloody-minded persistence is what got me through.

Performing with Mo actually took many more hours of practice than I needed for my solo performances, but the results were fantastic! We have had great deal of fun performing together on many occasions. Our audiences tell us that we make a great double act. We have expanded and crafted our act into an after dinner routine that has seen us working not only in the UK, but internationally. More about what happened follows in Chapter 10.

My First Paid Speaking Engagement

In my efforts to find work as an Optician when I first got back to the UK, I went to a meeting led by Sightcare – a company that supports independent practitioners. I thought it would be a good way to network and perhaps make some contacts that could lead to work.

The first person I saw when I arrived was Peter Sharpe – someone I knew from years before when I worked in London. I told him all about my trip to Australia and my discovery of a passion for speaking.

I told him that apart from working as an Optician, I wanted to make a difference to communication within our industry. I explained my amazement and frustration about the different way customers and staff treated me depending upon the role that I was in. I had worked in every role from receptionist through to clinician and had seen people's views passed over with no opportunity to contribute their insights and knowledge to the growth of the business. I spoke about my desire to open people's eyes to make more use of the potential available.

"Really?" he said. "'I want you to come over here and say that again to this person."

Peter didn't tell me who 'this person' was; I was just presented to a man and asked to repeat what I had said.

As I finished, he smiled at me and introduced himself as Paul Surridge, the Managing Director of Sightcare. He said that he was currently planning his list of speakers for their conference next year and asked if I would like to be one of them.

I accepted the challenge and set about creating a speech. As my nerves and imagination started getting the better of me, I was just at the point of calling to say I had changed my mind when the brochure for the conference arrived on my doorstep. Reading through the glossy pages and seeing my photo and speech title in bold print, knowing it had been sent out to all the delegates, there was no backing out.

Over the next three months, there was lots of preparation. I practised presenting before all sorts of people, in many different locations, including to the professional speakers that I knew. My final rehearsal was to two friends on a flight back from Majorca, the night before the event. I leaned over the back of the chair and presented to them, much to the laughter and entertainment of the young lads in the row behind them. Having to concentrate and keep going in spite of their merriment was great practice and made the real thing much easier to deal with.

When I was finally before the audience of 350 people, there were a few fluttering butterflies in my stomach, but it was mainly excitement that I felt – like a kid on my way to a birthday party!

All the practise and polishing of the performance paid off and it went brilliantly. The feedback from the speech was fantastic. People had said that they would go away and make sure that staff meetings gave everyone a chance to contribute, that they would be willing to talk to more people about the challenges before them and look for greater contribution from all members of staff. I felt that I really had made a positive difference.

With a goal in sight, the actions you take will go way beyond what you could achieve without an objective. Once you learn that you can take giant strides forward, the sky is the limit!

Without willingness to accept challenges from other people:

- I would never have got around to writing, practising and performing the presentation I gave at the Sightcare conference;
- After-dinner entertainment would never have entered my mind as a possibility;
- I can't imagine that I would ever have chosen to put myself through seven solo piano performances within a concert setting.

Some of you may ask, 'Does that mean you don't take action unless you have a big goal?' No, but I have to say that once I had started to take action, it was much easier to keep the ball rolling and continue to do so. Once the momentum stops, it can be slow and painful to start again.

What's The Piano in Your Life?

What specific goals could you set for yourself linked to something that you feel passionate about? The skills that will push you through your comfort zones will increase your levels of self-confidence and belief. This will pay dividends across the whole of your life. It is only through stepping beyond the boundaries that you already know, that you can discover more of your innate talent. Accepting challenges from other people can enable that growth to be greater and faster than you might envisage alone.

In the past you may have accepted challenges and followed a goal with great success. I am sure you remember the thrill of achievement! If you are feeling a bit stagnant right now, another challenge could be just what you need to get the momentum going again.

How high are you willing to allow someone else to set the high jump pole for you?

Do you have a clear idea of what goal you aspire to?

Do you have a strong enough reason 'why' you want to achieve it?

The next chapter will give you a few pointers that may help answer these questions and lead you to your own version of an inspiring 'piano' challenge.

Summary

- Have a specific goal in mind.

- Know what you want to achieve, and by when.

- Be willing to accept a greater challenge.

- Be willing to take on someone else's greater belief in your abilities.

5 | What's the Piano in Your Life?

'Do you pass on your passion or do you pass, on your passion?
Charles Kovess

I read this in a newsletter from Charles Kovess, a motivational speaker who I met at the Speakers Convention in Adelaide, Australia. He commented that the difference in grammar is small but the implication for the quality of life that we experience is huge.

A passion, a purpose and a jolly good reason why you want to achieve something is the fuel that you need to drive you towards your goal. That goal, however, doesn't always have to be about money, work or family. At times you need to do something just for yourself to refuel your sense of wellbeing. What might seem like an indulgence may actually be the key that provides you with more energy, self-belief and enthusiasm to achieve so much more in other areas of your life. For many people, though, passions lay unfulfilled, not fully expressed, or stuck in a closet hidden behind reasons like not enough time, not enough money, or with the blame at someone else's feet for why they can't achieve it.

When you are inspired by some great purpose ... all your thoughts break your bonds: your mind transcends limitations, your consciousness expands in every direction, and you find yourself in a new, great and wonderful world. Dormant forces, faculties and talents

*become alive, and you discover yourself to be a greater
person than you ever dreamed yourself to be.*

Patanjali (c.2nd century BC)
Ancient Indian philosopher and author of Yoga Sutras

Nick Williams, author of *The Work We Were Born To Do*, comments that most of us have become so used to listening to the instructions and opinions of others that we no longer have a clear idea of what we want to do. He asks us to consider what needs to happen for us to be willing to make a change.

John-Roger and Peter McWilliams comment in their book, *DO IT!*, that what we really want is often hidden beneath what we've settled for. When the comfort zone doesn't allow the expanded behaviour necessary to fulfil our dream, we tend to forget the dream.

Are there things in your life that you have been promising yourself that you will get around to one day? We've all said it at some point.

Advantages of Following a Passion

There are many advantages to be had from having an avenue to express and follow your passion. You will feel more joy, happiness, fulfilment, and contentment. You will be more creative in your outlook; you will surprise yourself with the qualities that you discover in yourself. You will feel more alive and in charge of your destiny as you find yourself with more energy. You will be liked by more people as you project a happier and more contented 'self'. Feeling happier will improve your body's immune system and leave you healthier in the body as well as the mind.

I had no qualms about chasing my passion for playing a piano as a child. I hadn't, at that time, developed the adult quality of trying to bury a dream or modify it to fit in with what someone else might find acceptable. When I no longer had a piano close to hand, the importance of playing and the pleasure that it provided became a distant memory.

Sometimes our 'hot buttons' are pressed when we see someone else doing what we secretly wish for ourselves. Feelings of jealousy are a sure indication of an unfulfilled desire. In Chapter 1, I mentioned how this became a sore point when I heard that my friend was going to live out my Australian dream before I had.

Richard Nelson Bolles, author of *What Color Is Your Parachute?*, talks about the virtue of passion or enthusiasm, and he comments:

> *Hold onto all of your dream. Most people don't find their heart's desire, because they decide to pursue just half their dream – consequently they hunt for it with only half their heart.*

Finding Your Passion

Some of you may be thinking that you are not sure what you are passionate about and wonder how you find a passion.

Jo Parfitt, author of *Find Your Passion*, suggests looking to our past successes, as they can often hold clues to our buried passions.

Take a few moments to consider your answers to these questions:

What do you truly enjoy and feel inspired by?

What gives you the experience of joy?

Where is your passion and motivation at the moment?

What would you love to do if you had all the time and money that you needed?

What are you good at?

What comes naturally to you?

What are you doing when you lose all track of time?

What are your strongest interests?

If you were content to be a beginner, what would you learn to do?

Sometimes it is only by picking up a long-lost hobby that we get to discover what it once provided for us.

Sometimes it is only when you are willing to change a routine and try something completely different, that you can discover hidden talents and what you might be capable of. This may well provide a refreshing new source of pleasure in your life.

Changing the Environment

Feeling energised and revitalised by a holiday has a lot to do with changing a routine and doing new and inspiring things. Taking up a new hobby can have the same effect.

Changing your surroundings can make new behaviour seem more like an easily accessible option. Often when you go on holiday, you will be inspired by a new environment. What options would you explore just for the fun of it? Imagine what you might be looking into if you were able to bring that holiday mentality to your everyday life. Having an inquisitive nature will provide you with more options.

When was the last time that you did something for the first time?

We can get so entrenched in having to be good at something to derive enjoyment from it, that it is easy to forget the core life-skills that can be polished by learning a new skill - like patience, persistence, and not being put off when things don't instantly go right. Discovering a new skill can only come about if we are willing to be a beginner.

While I was living in North Queensland (before the crash), one of the patients I examined was an art teacher. During her eye examination, as I carefully worked out the power her glasses needed to be for her to be able to paint at arms' length, she mentioned to me that, in her opinion, she could teach anyone to paint. I saw this as an opportunity and a challenge, so I asked if I could be her next student. Painting was not something that I had aspired to do and had not been a forte at school. In my mind I was useless at drawing. She was eager to teach me and I was eager to learn.

She showed me lots of books with paintings in them. I was asked to pick one that inspired me. I chose a picture of a frog-mouth owl. I liked all the different shades of brown contrasted by the bright orange colour in his eyes. When I presented it to her, she asked, "Are you sure? Is there another picture that you really liked but were afraid to say so?" She was very perceptive; the scene that I really liked was of a purple and yellow sunset with foaming sea crashing over rocks, throwing white froth up towards the sky. She smiled as she looked at it and said, "Well, that's not where I would usually start, but if that's what inspires you then that's what we'll do."

I really enjoyed the lessons. The feeling that I got from the concentration and calmness of being focused and still, reminded me of how I used to feel after playing a piano. I had never had a hobby that gave me that same sensation until then. The result that I achieved astounded me. When I had finished the painting, I commented to her that it wasn't really my talent on the canvas, as she had shown me what to do at every stage. Her question back to me was,

When your mother taught you to walk, did you think that you couldn't really walk?

My newfound talent and passion for painting has taken a back seat since then, but I am glad that I took the opportunity to try something new. I look forward to when I choose to spend more time exploring that avenue. I am curious to find out how far I can take it.

If you have followed your passion, have you toned it down to fit in with what you think other people will consider acceptable?

Some people will take the essence of what it was that they wanted to do and live out their dreams through others. For example, the father who always wanted to play football as a youngster, but never had the opportunity, who ploughs his passion and enthusiasm into running a team for local school children. These people are great at passing on their enthusiasm to others.

Or the parent, who always wanted to go to drama school, but never got there, who decides to send their children to one from an early age. This is not always so well received! I know many parents who always wanted to play a piano who force their children to learn when they have no interest of their own. This is more likely to have the reverse of the intended effect and leave the child hating music lessons.

In all of these examples, the desire and motivation stem from unrequited passion.

Some parents put all of their own desires on hold because of their children. The child can never repay this debt of time, and I wonder if there might be more of the real essence of the parent available for the child, if they were willing to keep a little time and an outlet of passion in their own lives too.

There are many advantages for you to take forward into the rest of your life if you are willing to identify and follow your passion. Ask yourself what has to change for you to be willing to take action.

Dust off those buried dreams and desires and use what you find within the pages of this book to turn the thought 'one day I'm going to ...' into 'I'm working on that!', or better still, 'WOW, done that, what next?'

You never know what talent is lying dormant, just waiting for you to find it and make use of it!

Summary

- Identify the ending of the following sentence for you – 'One day I'm going to ...'.

- Make a note of all the things that give you a sense of passion and inspiration.

- Do something about it!

6 Boost Your Belief

You are not what you think you are; what you think, you are.

Anon

When I was young I knew nothing about the concept of beliefs and why or how they came about. I never questioned the reasoning behind the belief that I couldn't play the piano in public, that I wasn't good at chemistry, or that I was useless at writing essays. I wasn't aware at the time, that these and many other thoughts were self-imposed, limiting beliefs. I simply believed them to be true.

Changing my view from, 'I can't play the piano in public', to now being able to sit down and confidently play whenever asked, didn't happen overnight. Shifting that belief comes from all that I talk about in this book, but there is also a psychological aspect to managing the thought process, which allows you to take the steps to change it in the first place.

The way I made myself take that action was by establishing a goal that I was determined to reach. The consequences of not reaching my target were worse in my mind than the stress that I needed to go through to get beyond the fear and self-doubt.

In Chapter 4 I talked about the challenge set for me by Steve McDermott – to play the piano to introduce his presentation at the Professional Speakers conference. Knowing that Steve was relying on me took my reason for success and my purpose beyond being just about me. By taking the actions necessary to reach that goal, I gathered the proof necessary to change my belief about my ability for good.

When you first fly in the face of a limiting belief and achieve positive results, it leaves you with an amazing feeling of confidence and self-assurance. Disproving the 'I can't' thought that had previously kicked in on automatic pilot, opened up a whole new world of possibilities that I found really challenging, exciting and full of potential.

The **good news** – When you put into practice the techniques to change one limiting belief, you gain the skills necessary to change any others.

The **bad news** – Once you have proved to yourself what you are capable of, it's uncomfortable to accept any less from yourself!

Noticing that there are limits in your mind is the first step to being able to change the thoughts that hold you back. It is important to change them, as a limiting belief will always precede a limiting decision. Having a planned strategy to boost your belief will help to ensure that your **COMMITMENT** remains greater than your **concerns** as you strive for your goal.

95% of what we do in life is the result of a developed habit. Research shows that, to change a habit, we have to do something differently for 21 consecutive days for the new action to become automatic. So just deciding to change the belief isn't enough – there has to be consistent action to back it up. By taking consistent action towards your goal, the cement is laid around the foundation stones of a new, empowering, and chosen belief about your ability.

Understanding Beliefs

The Intention Of The Limiting Belief

Think of a time when you have wanted to do something and then countered it with the thought, 'I can't because I'm ...' or 'Yes, but ...' and talked yourself out of it. We're often afraid to start something for fear of not being good enough, or fearing failure. The thoughts that warn us of impending potential failure can see us walk away from opportunities. This is the result of our subconscious trying to protect us from defeat. This is often termed 'protecting your comfort zone'.

Recognising The Patterns

We often react to situations because of what has happened in the past. Those events can affect the way that we think and the actions that we take, whether or not the pattern is still relevant. You may have heard the story about the cat that burnt itself on the hot stove and never went anywhere near a stove again, whether it was on or not. How often do you choose your pursuits based on the same reasoning as the cat?

If you judge your capabilities on what has gone before, you will live your life constrained by your beliefs about what you can achieve based on that evidence. The way you picture yourself in the future is also a reflection of these limitations.

You might have constantly been told as a youngster that you were no good at maths. Once you have heard this kind of sentence a few times, it can be embedded as a belief that is carried forward into the future, no matter how limiting and perhaps incorrect it may be. It can be difficult to break out of such a belief. Our subconscious does a great job of protecting our beliefs whether they are helpful or not!

Imagine what it would be like if you were to wipe away those limiting thoughts and associations. You could choose a new and more appropriate behaviour instead of reacting based on your past experiences. Your abilities would increase dramatically as a direct result.

I admire clever use of language and I remember the first time I saw Clive Gott, a motivational 'entertrainer' talk about the word BELIEF. He wrote the word in bold letters on a flip chart, and then crossed out the first two letters and the last one, leaving the word LIE. His implication was that sometimes a belief that we have, may in fact contain a lie.

He also introduced me to the simple transformation of the word IMPOSSIBLE to I'M POSSIBLE.

Keep this in mind as you start to challenge your thinking.

Counting The Cost

Have you considered what the emotional and financial cost is to you of continuing to live under the rule of a limiting belief? It will have a powerful impact on the way that your future will turn out.

Robin Norwood puts it very well in the pages of *Women Who Love Too Much* –

> *Consider the cost of not acting. You will probably blame your nearest and dearest as being the reason for your lack of development. That resentment can eat away at your relationship. I am sure that you would not wish for your partner to not develop to his best ability because he is with you. The cookie cuts both ways.*

Are you guilty of blaming someone else for your lack of progress?

Paving The Way For An Empowering Belief

In order to change a belief, we must first become aware of the limitation and then take steps which disprove it.

First, recognise what limiting belief it is that you want to change and feed your subconscious something to replace it. When the negative, limiting thought comes to the front of your mind, you need a counter attack. If, like me, you've been telling yourself for years that you can't do something – in my case, play a piano in public – you'll need to find a strong, positive statement to replace that – 'I can play the piano well'. If that's way beyond what you are willing to consider as an option, try starting with something like, 'My confidence in my ability grows stronger every day'. It's even better if you have more description, i.e., 'When I play the piano, everyone likes to listen and enjoys my music'. The more frequently you programme this thought into your mind, the more believable it will become.

By reinforcing your chosen belief, your subconscious will eventually start seeing this as reality. In this way, your subconscious will work with you rather than against you so that you continue to take action instead of continuously providing reasons why you can't.

When you start taking action to change the belief, somewhere along the line, your state of mind about that belief will change from one of 'fake it till you make it,' to a feeling of confidence and certainty in your ability.

For example, when you first learn to drive everything is difficult, because you haven't done it before. As you learn, your ability and skills improve, and you become more aware of what you can and can't yet easily do. Once you master the skill, you can put the actions into practice without having to think about them. Your belief changes from, 'I can't drive,' to 'I can drive.'

Recognisable Stages of Transition

As your skills progress, your awareness and ability will go through stages. You will discover there are

Things that you know.

Things that you know that you don't know.

And things you don't know that you don't know.

A well-known model takes you from:

Unconscious Incompetence:
I don't know that I don't know.

Think of a novice golfer – they've never picked up a golf club so don't have the first idea what they will need to do to learn. Left to themselves, they may be able to swing the club, but it's very unlikely that they will do this correctly.

Conscious Incompetence:
I know what I don't know and notice the mistakes that I make and am aware of what I need to learn.

This is the stage where the novice golfer has now had a lesson from the pro and is struggling to get it right. This is the point where some golfers throw their clubs in the river!

Conscious Competence:
I know what I'm doing and can do it well when I think about it.

With some more lessons and practice our golfer can now swing accurately, providing that he carefully makes sure that his feet, arms and club are all in the 'right' position first.

Unconscious Competence:
I can carry out the activity without consciously thinking about it.

The golfer can now stroll onto the tee, set up his ball, line up and concentrate on where he wants the ball to go without having to worry about being in the 'right' position; he just does it naturally.

My piano skills were at the 'conscious incompetence' level before I took on this challenge. It took a great deal of practice to get to 'conscious competence'. I have arrived at the 'unconscious competence' level with a few pieces of music, but it will still take lots of practice before other pieces are at the concert performance stage.

How to Challenge and Change The Belief

Change The Reference Points

To change a belief you must change the reference points that underpin it. This change of your mindset alone can make the difference between success and failure. There are plenty of examples from history of how a change in belief has affected performance and outcomes:

- When new medicines are tried out, some people take the real treatment and others take a placebo (a pill with no active ingredient). Curiously, those who take a placebo have an increased recovery rate because of their belief that they will get better due to the medication that they think they are taking.

111

- For years it was said that it was impossible to run a mile in under 4 minutes. The year after Roger Bannister broke that record, 356 other people around the world also managed to run the distance in under 4 minutes.

- When a stage hypnotist sets to work and has people acting with great confidence in areas that would normally make them squirm, we have clear evidence of how beliefs would normally prevent those abilities from shining so brightly.

Talented School Children Or Not?

A negative view of someone's ability has been shown to limit the potential outcome of achievement for that person. Brian Tracy in his tape series, *The Psychology of Achievement*, recounts the story about a group of teachers who were told they had school children with high ability compared to the rest of the school and that they had been assigned these gifted children as a reward for their hard work. At the end of the year, these students outperformed other classes across all subjects. It was then revealed that there was no difference in their abilities, they had not been hand-picked, but that they were part of an experiment to demonstrate the power of having belief in a person and how that belief affects other people's performance.

Table Tops and Santa Claus

When Steve McDermott gave his opening presentation at the Professional Speakers conference about belief and how you can change it, the metaphor that he used to illustrate beliefs was of a table: the tabletop representing the belief, and the four legs that support it representing the reasons behind why we hold the belief.

He told a story about his children and their belief in Santa Claus (or otherwise). In his analogy the legs of the table represent the reasons why his children and we would have held the belief about Santa Claus being real. Leg 1 – presents arrive on Christmas Day; Leg 2 – our teachers talked about Christmas time at school; Leg 3 – we would see cards and decorations all over the place; and Leg 4 – meeting Santa in person in the shops before the big day.

Once we discover that Santa isn't real, the 'table top' (belief) changes. The legs that now support the new belief come from the discovery that it was Dad who dressed up in the Santa costume, that it was our parents who put the presents under the tree, that the teachers were in on the story, and so too, was everyone else. Our belief changed because our references changed.

In order to change the belief that you hold about yourself, you need to change the reference points you adopt and then choose the most empowering, positive thoughts about your abilities. You will need to gather evidence of success and take actions that support the new belief for it to become a reality.

Nick Williams, author of *The Work We Were Born To Do*, suggests that we need to be willing to see ourselves with new eyes.

Help From Professionals
Seeking help from a trained professional can speed up the process when tackling issues of limiting beliefs. There are many types of practitioners from many different arenas available to help you with this, from psychotherapists, to hypnotherapists, cognitive behavioural therapists and NLP practitioners. All of these knowledgeable professionals use slightly different techniques to help you deal with issues and move you forward with a greater confidence in your ability to succeed. Often, they will offer a free, short initial consultation so that you can meet them to see if you think you can work together. If you choose to include this route as part of your action plan, do your research and get a personal recommendation if you can.

Fake It Till You Make It

When you are taking steps to reach your goal, act as if you are confident and already have the new belief that would support you in place. If you find it hard to think or act in that way, call on resources and help from elsewhere. Refer back to your list of people who can help you and ask for support. You don't have to have all the answers about how that support could be given. Be willing to let people know that you need help in order to take the action.

Consider that life is a bit like a game of snakes and ladders – the aim is to get to number 100. That is where you will have proved your worth, completed your challenges and celebrated your success. Realistically, en route to number 100, there will be times when you slide down the snake and find yourself back in a place where you have already been. Having people to help support the belief will enable you to climb back up the ladders more easily.

Set Goals and Take Action

As I mentioned in Chapter 4, aiming for defined goal posts will ensure directional and congruent action steps.

Those steps need to be measurable and achievable in the beginning. As your courage and confidence grows, make the steps and the stretch for you between those goals larger and more challenging, in line with the expanding self-belief.

There were definite transition phases for me. I started by making the commitment to play a piano wherever I saw one. This progressed and I continued to expand my comfort zone by having audiences listening, first at home and then in more formal environments. I also went through the discipline of recording what was I doing so that I could listen back to it and improve on the weaker aspects. By increasing the pressure gradually in this way, I bolstered the belief in my ability to perform in a concert environment. Even then, gaining experience in that environment could only be done once I had an event at which to perform. These were the essential building blocks on the road to changing the initial limiting belief.

Gather Evidence

As a result of the steps that I took, I was able to gather evidence of progress and of success, which defied the initial limiting belief about my ability to play the piano in public. With your own challenge, have you identified what the evidence is that has you believe a certain way? Take a look at my example and note down for yourself what your evidence is.

Belief – 'I Can't Play The Piano in Public'

Evidence For	Evidence Against
I knew that I disappointed my parents by not being able to play for them as a youngster	At school I knew I was good at music. I did so well playing a recorder that I was moved up to play with the kids in the year above me. I believed that I was good at playing the recorder.
I froze with embarrassment when asked to play for my family at my grandma's house. (see Chapter 2)	I was good at playing the guitar. When I started the guitar it didn't bother me too much when I was asked to play for other people.
Every music exam that I took, I barely scraped a pass as the nerves got hold of me. In an exam situation I was never able to play a piece of music as well as I knew I could at home, when no one was listening.	When I had played the piano for people when I was in Melbourne, it didn't matter that I had made mistakes. I proved that, with practice, I could improve and that my playing inspired other people.

As you gather evidence of progress and success, add this to your column 'Evidence Against!' Soon the scales will be tipped in the favour of your new belief that says 'I can', rather than 'I can't'.

Another way I found useful to bolster my belief was to call on examples from the past where I had broken through areas that I found challenging. The following chemistry story is a great example for me, which I always bear in mind as I face up to a challenge where I might doubt my ability to succeed.

Chemistry Challenge

When I was at University studying to become an Optician, I struggled with the chemistry aspect of the course, as I didn't have an 'A' level in this subject. I was the bane of the chemistry teacher's life, because I was always asking questions about things that didn't seem logical to me. One day, I couldn't read his writing on the board to tell whether he had written an N or an H, so I asked and was yelled at with the words, 'If you don't understand it, see me after class!'

I didn't go to him for help. I went to one of my housemates from the halls of residence, who was studying a pure chemistry degree. He was happy to help me out and explain some basics. To be able to learn the many difficult formulas, I would invent memorable, funny and rude sayings that followed the initials in the equations. I don't recall specifically what they were, but they were so good that my chemistry friend even used a couple of them for his revision! Anyway, back to the story, we were asked to learn the chemical configuration of the 21 amino acids. This is what one looks like:

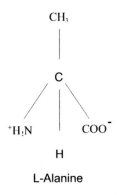

L-Alanine

There are 21 of these things to learn, and they all looked very similar. I remember the professor's reasoning for this – he said that it was to teach us that we can learn anything if we really want to. I SLOGGED to learn these. I thought, at the time, it would be a lot more practical use for me to learn the numbers from a page in the telephone directory, because I might, at least, need one of them one day.

It was so difficult for me that I had to I apply myself more than I had ever done in the past to be able to memorise it. To my horror, in the exam, the question about it didn't come up. I was livid! I wrote them all out on the back of the exam paper anyway just to prove a point, and I ended up with chemistry being my second highest exam mark.

My tutor told me that you could have knocked the professor over with a feather when he saw my mark. To say I disliked him at the time would be an understatement! But I know that the lesson he taught me was a valuable one. I know that when I tackle a piece of music, or any aspect that seems initially beyond my reach, if I am willing to take it one step at a time and work on it, I will eventually get it. It may take years, and that is how I got to play the piece of music called *Robin's Return*, so I have it in my kit bag to use and offer it to you with proof that hard work can pay off.

Since those days, I have learnt other techniques like mind mapping and association techniques that would have helped me to memorise with more efficiency. If you need some guidance in advancing your skills in that area, please take a look at the Resource section and contact Michael Tipper or Henry Hopking.

> *A person with average abilities can outstrip a person with great ability if determination is there.*
>
> Brian Tracy

Manage Your Self-Talk

You may receive love and support from the people around you but all that can end in self-sabotage if you are not willing to offer positive words of support to yourself. What you say to yourself can have a huge impact on your likelihood of success.

This voice that you use to either admonish or encourage yourself is often known as the 'inner critic'.

> *If I said to my friends what I say to myself, I wouldn't have any friends!*
>
> Princess Diana

Are you able to catch yourself when you call yourself stupid or when you compare yourself unfavo urably to others?

Do you do anything to change it apart from hope and wish?

Notice what it is that you say to yourself about why you aren't doing what you say you want to do. Catch yourself when you put yourself down or have negative thoughts about an event. If you write these thoughts down each time they come to mind, you will be able to see on paper how often your thoughts are poisoning your mind. For the next 24 hours, be aware of this voice and notice how often it is positive and how often it is negative. The proportion given to each may help you to see an area where more support could, with practice, be forthcoming.

An exercise to practise from cognitive behavioural therapy:

- Write down all the comments that you say to yourself through the day.

- Note when you say this, and if it is positive or negative.

Write down something to encourage and support you that counteracts the negative thought.

Using this exercise will interrupt the usual thought pattern. This will help you to banish those negative voices in your head telling you what you can't do and allow you to replace them with positive thoughts that will help you rather than hinder your progress.

A more advanced version might also make note of where you were or who you were with so that you can see the association between certain situations and associated thought processes.

For Example

Times of Day	Location	Thought	Positive/ Negative	More appro-priate and encouraging thought
7.20am	In bed	Why am I do-ing this? It's ridiculous to be putting myself through this much stress; it's not going to achieve any-thing!	Negative	I am really proud that I am learning about expanding my comfort zone. Michael will help me to focus my mind before the concert. I am doing a brave and courageous thing.
8.00am	Leaving for work	You're so stupid; why didn't you check the door lock before driving away? You can't even do some-thing as simple as that!	Negative	OK, so you are not sure if you locked the door. You have a lot on your mind at the moment. It's really important to be in the moment and think about each thing as you do it. Take your time. You can do it!

I thought that once I had conquered the fear and had an attitude of 'I can' or 'I will find a way to do this', that my negative voices would disappear forever. I was looking forward to taking on each new challenge without feeling like I was driving with the hand brake on. I was wrong.

Writing this book, for example, has produced many such occasions when I have had to relearn all of the enclosed wisdom of this book. I have often had to remind myself how to quieten the voice that says, 'That's not good enough' or 'What makes you think you can be a writer?' Susan Jeffers in her highly acclaimed book, *Feel the Fear and Do It Anyway*, remarks that the doubting voice never goes away, but that we have to learn to hear it in a different way.

A technique that I learnt on a Tony Robbins course helps to reduce the impact of the negative voice. In the world of Neuro-linguistic programming (NLP) this technique is known as experimenting with sub modalities.

Notice:

What is it that you say to yourself?

Where in your mind you hear it – does the voice speak from behind you, or into your left or right ear?

In what sort of tone do you hear the voice – does it sound like your mother, or a stern old teacher?

When you have identified these answers:

- Project that voice to another position; for example, if you heard it from the left at the height of your ear, project it to the right and coming up from the floor below you.

- Speed up the words and make it sound really stupid like the voice of a cartoon. For example – hear it like the voice of Daffy Duck or Porky Pig.

I know this sounds weird, but give it a go! It worked for me and seemed to have great effect for the other 8,999 people in the audience. With a little practice at this technique, you will end up laughing when you hear the voice of doubt, and your power and ability to act in the direction that you want to will increase ten-fold.

Manage Your Environment

If your environment is a reflection of your new way of thinking and relating to yourself, you are providing evidence of it as a reality. More often than not, the environment gives away your true relationship with yourself.

Our mental state can be affected by the power of suggestion from the environment, e.g., if I have a messy car and a messy house, it can be the evidence and basis of the belief – I'm an untidy person. If you can relate to this scenario, you may not even have been aware of how your environment influenced this. With my new belief about my ability to be tidy, for example, coming home to my usual mess will not help me to work on the new belief (just a little reminder to myself!). Clearing it up and falling into old habits again will also not help. Taking a little bit of decisive action each day is more likely to lead to success. Sound familiar?

At the times when I was making the most progress to change my belief about my ability to play the piano in public, then 'my game' so to speak, picked up in all other areas of my life.

How you do anything is how you do everything! Is how I once heard it described.

Brian Tracy, the motivational speaker that I mentioned earlier, claims that 95% of what you do is determined by suggestive and psychological influences around you. A kind word from someone can cause you to feel happy for the rest of the day, whereas a rude word from a fellow driver on your way to work might put you in a bad mood for the day.

We all have hot buttons that cause a habitual reaction to a negative stimulus. You may respond to external suggestion from depressing stories on the TV or on the radio, or from books, comments from your family, queues of traffic or the miserable weather. You think that you are 'acting', but often it is reacting. When you are in control of your emotions, you can choose to be happy despite the environment.

Acting as if you are confident and already have the new belief firmly in place can overwrite the old belief by producing feelings consistent with the new belief. The more supportive evidence that you are able to gather, the more stable the new belief will be.

Have a Visual Reminder

A visual reminder can help you to bypass and reinforce your belief in your ability to succeed. By having something tangible that has a bigger meaning than the object itself, like a picture or an ornament, it can help to remind you of your focus, your determination and your goal. This can work even if the image or picture is in your head, but it has more impact if it is an object in reality. I had two aspects that filled this role for me.

During the year of physiotherapy after the car crash, the image that I kept in my mind was of me playing a piano piece. It was one that my music teacher, Mrs Hind, used to play at the end of my lessons. I had learnt only part of it when I learnt to play as a child, but I was always inspired by the thought that one day I would be able to play it as well as she could. I kept telling myself that my hand would get better and I would be able to play the piano again. The pain I endured during those physiotherapy sessions was anaesthetised in part by such thoughts.

As I travelled around Australia during my camper van tour, my visit to Sydney included a shopping trip to the sales. I came across a little designer boutique tucked away in a back street that was closing down. Everything had been reduced up to four times, much too tempting to resist!

On the central rack I found a stunning, sparkly cropped top edged in black beads and covered with sequins in square patterns in shades of gold, bronze, white, and black and lined with black silk. It was really heavy to pick up because of all the beadwork. The way it caught the light was beautiful. Its original price was A$845 (about £325). That price had been crossed out and so had two others. Now the red pen on the tag read A$100 (that's an amazingly cheap £40).

As I held it in my hands an image flashed in my mind. I saw myself on a stage in front of a huge audience playing a piano wearing the sparkly top. As I went back to my lessons and began to push myself to play in front of other people, I held this image in my mind. I had the top, so I had to make the image I had seen a reality. Having seen it, I believed it. What you see on the front cover is the top I am referring to, and I did indeed wear it when I performed in some of the concerts that you will read about in Chapter 10.

Tim Gallwey and Barry Green authors of the book, *The Inner Game of Music*, share a story about a famous American tenor called James McCracken. When he was in his late teens, he posted a small star in a corner of his bathroom mirror. He told the authors that every morning when he went to shave, that star would remind him of his life's goal – to sing at the Metropolitan Opera. He also made that image a reality.

I have a good friend, Nicky Slater, who is a skating champion from the Torvill and Dean era. He told me that when it came to competition time, after the warm up sessions while the UK team sat in the dressing rooms waiting for the time to pass, Katrina Witt (Olympic gold medalist figure skating champion in1984 and 1988) was taken out to shop for the dress that she would wear at the gala dinner to celebrate her anticipated and assumed victory. So by the time Katrina stepped onto the ice to compete, she had already seen in her mind her entrance to the party as the victorious champion.

Put Your Goals Onto A Card and Re-Read Many Times A Day

Having a specific measurable outcome broken down into achievable chunks will boost your belief about your ability to reach your goal. Reminding yourself often of what it is that you want, will speed your actions towards progress. You could put this in your wallet and each time you remove one of your cards, as you see it you will be reminded of your intention.

At times when I am pushing hard to reach a goal, I will have a Post-it® Note in the centre of my steering wheel on my car that reminds me of my goal. On it will be written what specifically it is that I want to achieve. The time that I then spend driving puts my thinking time to greater use as I apply myself to think about the challenge and plan how I am going to do it. As I achieve the goal, the Post-it® Note gets changed.

What form of prompt or reminder would help you to keep your mind focused on your challenge?

What message would be relevant for you to have on your steering wheel?

Repeat Positive Messages to Yourself

Not everyone may be instantly open to the idea of affirmations or the belief that they can work, but Dr Seligman at the University of Pennsylvania has discovered that high performers talk to themselves very differently compared to low performing people. He also remarks that your self-talk determines your inner quality of life.

A verbal antidote to fear of failure would be to repeat to yourself, 'I can do it, I can do it!' Affirmations need to be present tense, personal and positive in nature to have the greatest impact. Repetition in all forms whether verbal, visually imagined or action orientated will help to reinforce a pattern of action and of having belief in yourself. Even if you don't believe what you are saying in the beginning, the effect on your subconscious can be very powerful. With time and repetition, the mantra will have a positive impact on your subconscious, which in turn, will impact how you think and feel about yourself. Ultimately changing for the better, the actions that you take as a result of that belief.

Get Creative with your own positive messages
You can extend this idea a little further by having a positive saying to greet you when you switch on your phone. Something like:

BELIEVE IN YOU!

YOU WILL SUCCEED!

GO FOR IT!

On my phone it currently says, 'Be your own best friend!' This reminds me to be as kind and compassionate to myself as I would be to a good friend, avoiding the tendency to work until I drop and then berate myself for not having achieved everything on my 'TO DO' list.

Visualise Your Outcome
By imagining the outcome that you want to achieve, you will be getting your body and your thoughts used to a certain pattern of events. Athletes use this technique every time they compete. In their minds they have won the impending event again and again. The more emotion that you use as you visualise, the more it influences how fast it will emerge in your reality.

Be creative; get thinking! If it works for me, it can work for you too!

How many times do you have to do something before you believe you really can do it?

I remember being intrigued when this question was put to me by my friend Gihan Perera, whom I met when I attended the course *Speak for Money* that I mentioned earlier. He was one of the guest speakers – being an expert in the field of creating leverage for profit. He finds hidden income opportunities in businesses.

Gihan and I were talking over the phone when I was back in the UK, about the piano concerts that I was performing in. He asked how many times I would need to perform in a concert before I would know that I could easily play a piano in public. I didn't know the answer at the time and I still don't. I had to take the action and provide evidence that supported the new belief for it to become real. I've played now many times in public. There wasn't one event where the belief suddenly changed, but I think that the question is a really useful one to put to yourself when you set yourself a challenge to change a belief.

What evidence or how much evidence will you need for you to believe that you can do 'it'?

Look For Inspiration

Over the years I am sure you have come across many things that make you feel inspired. Having a regular dose of inspiration can help provide the fuel to help you keep going on this journey of transformation and enhanced self-belief. So plan for it:

- Arrange to go to a concert and watch other people perform.
- Watch a film with an inspiring story line.
- Visit a festival.
- Take time to watch an inspiring story on the TV.

Work some inspiration into your plan! Spend more time with those in your network who believe in you, learning by osmosis and taking on another person's belief in you can help you to help you to realise greater potential more quickly and with greater assurance. As you expand your capabilities and strive to achieve more, there may be people in your circle whom you choose not to spend time with because of the negative impact they have on you. If a person is a constant drain on your energy, then you may not wish to associate with them at a time when you know you need to bolster your resources rather than deplete them.

My piano teacher, Maria, taught me a very valuable lesson about belief one afternoon. She caught me in my tracks; not believing in my abilities. I was playing part of a piece of music that I had set my heart on learning – *Clair de Lune* by Debussy. It's a haunting, relaxing tune, almost trance-like in its progression. At times it has eight notes being played each time you hear a single chord as part of the melody. The mechanics of playing this amount of notes at one stretch is a real challenge for my hand, not only because of having to stretch so far but also because it is at the edge of my technical ability.

I was faltering halfway through and stopped midway and asked her if I had set myself a goal beyond my abilities and if I ought to be playing something easier. She looked down at me sternly and said with her charming Russian accent, "I am the teacher and I will tell you when you need to choose something easier to play. You just need to practise."

I felt humbled by this, but also disappointed in myself for not believing in my ability as much as she obviously did.

At first I chose to take on the opinion that others had of my abilities. It took time to develop my own strong supporting belief. The foundation of the new belief grew stronger as I made progress. Belief in my abilities was also bolstered by support from the network of people I had around me.

I had told so many people what I was up to that there was no room to contemplate backing out. They were all expecting me to be able to do what I set out to achieve.

Who do you know who absolutely believes in your ability to succeed?

Choose to take on their views about your capabilities.

Take Care of Yourself

Not everyone will provide you with the strengthening beliefs you need. Sometimes you have to be self-reliant. Sometimes you may not get any positive input to help you and, if you are dependant on someone loving you or voicing approval and you don't get what you need, it can hold you back. It's easy to be influenced by the environment, the weather, and how you happen to be feeling. You must be aware that if you allow this to happen, you are less likely to make progress.

What it boils down to is that you take 100 % responsibility for your own life – including what you allow to influence you and from where those influences come. Remember, you need to be your own best friend, and that means giving yourself the positive input that will keep you going and rejecting any negative input from others.

This not only applies to our belief, but also to the fundamental aspects of self-care. If you are not looking after yourself then making progress will be so much harder to achieve. Think of yourself like a car that needs careful maintenance. If you were to drive around in a vehicle that had been pushed to its limits, with a battery that was almost flat, and you didn't get the oil and water changed until something went wrong, you wouldn't expect the car to remain reliable. Compare that to one which is serviced regularly, is given suitable breaks between journeys and is topped up with oil and water on a regular basis. The car in the second option is a lot more likely to remain reliable and working when stretched. The same applies to you!

Are you getting enough sleep?

Are you eating really well?

Do you drink enough water?

Are you getting enough exercise?

Take care of the fundamentals!

As the proverb says,

If you always do what you've always done, you'll always get what you've always got!'

Capture The Insights

By writing down what's going on in your life in the pages of a diary or journal, you will be able to record the insights and lessons that you learn along the way. This will be a valuable record and a source book for your own success. After all, that is how this book began. We each have our own tried and tested blueprint for success, so why not capitalise on it.

Putting my thoughts on paper, I find, stops them churning around in my mind. I am much more likely to gain insight by taking action in this way. If I feel stuck on an issue, I think back to the strategies that I have outlined here, which I have proved to myself work, and I apply them. Taking a dose of my own medicine is what is often needed to get the ball rolling again.

Listen to Empowering Music

I mentioned in Chapter 2 how I met Jana Stanfield at the first National Speakers Conference that I went to in Adelaide. Her songs inspire and motivate you to succeed beyond the voices of doubt. There was one song in particular that really spoke to me. I replay it for real or from my memory whenever I need an extra dose of courage and belief. The words appear below with Jana's permission. Copies of her fantastically empowering albums can be found via her web site www.janastanfield.com

If I Were Brave By Jana Stanfield
> *What would I do if I knew that I could not fail?*
> *If I believed would the wind always fill up my sail?*
> *How far would I go, what could I achieve,*
> *Trusting the hero in me?*
>
> *If I were brave I'd walk the razor's edge,*
> *Where fools and dreamers dare to tread,*
> *And never lose faith, even when losing my way,*
> *What steps would I take, today, if I were brave?*
> *What would I do today if I were brave?*
>
> *What if we're all meant to do what we secretly dream?*
> *What would you ask if you knew you could have anything?*
> *Like the mighty oak sleeps in the heart of a seed,*
> *Are there miracles in you and me?*
>
> *If I were brave I'd walk the razor's edge,*
> *Where fools and dreamers dare to tread,*
> *And never lose faith, even when losing my way,*
> *What steps would I take, today, if I were brave?*
>
> *If I refuse to listen to the voice of fear,*
> *Would the voice of courage whisper in my ear?*
>
> *If I were brave I'd walk the razor's edge,*
> *Where fools and dreamers dare to tread,*
> *And never lose faith, even when losing my way,*
> *What steps would I take, today, if I were brave?*
> *What would I do today if I were brave?*

What's The Piano in Your Life?

On a journey that takes you out of your comfort zone, it is almost inevitable that there will be times when your belief deserts you or you feel really low. Do not fear this happening.

Be assured that this is normal! Practise the sk˙
act the negative self-talk. You have many oti.
call on, for example; get some help, call a friend
listen to a CD that inspires you, and then refer to C.
on practice.

There may be times when it is relevant and pertinent to seek the help of a professional to help lift your mood and further your understanding of what makes you tick.

Having read through this chapter, I am sure there are instances that have come to mind of times when you have doubted your ability. Know that it is possible for you to take some action and do something about it in order to help you move forward. Choose to act despite the interfering voices of doubt. Once you start to take action and see progress, you will be inspired to believe even more in your ability to succeed.

Take the time now to think how the sections in this chapter relate to you and which techniques you are going to try. This is the only way to find out what best works for you!

Once you start to move, make a note of the insights and lessons that you learn along the way. This will be valuable for you to call on when you meet your next big hurdle.

Questions to Consider:

What limiting beliefs do you need to work on?

What is the cost of those current beliefs?

What does your probable future look like if the beliefs remain that way?

What is the evidence that is contrary to the limiting belief?

What is your new chosen belief?

What benefits will be present in your life as a result?

What needs to change for you to begin to take action?

What is your evidence of past success that you will call on to boost your belief?

Who do you know who absolutely believes in your ability to succeed? Choose to take on their view about what you can do.

How many times do you need to do something before you will believe that you can do it?

Summary

- Have a goal, work steadily towards it; take action steps in bite-sized pieces.

- Record the progress as you go.

- Fake it till you make it – act as if you have confidence and belief in your ability.

- Manage your thought process, your language, and your environment. Make sure that they are all congruent with your chosen, positive belief.

- Look for inspiration.

- Make use of external tools that will help to support your belief, e.g. affirmations, visualisation, listening to empowering music.

- Take action and GO FOR IT!

7 | Practise, Practise, Practise

God gives talent, work transforms talent into genius.

Anna Pavlova

In my challenge to conquer my fear of playing the piano in public, the key to success was practice. Practice was not just sitting in front of the piano to learn the piece of music. The more challenging part of the 'practice' was practising the personal qualities like persistence, patience and discipline that made the practice effective.

None of us like it when we aren't very good at something. Human nature has us tend to favour doing things which come easily. We expect a certain standard of ourselves, and when we don't reach that we have two choices – we can either avoid the task by doing something else or we can choose to work at it.

When considering the topic of practice, ask yourself the question, 'What is the best way to bridge the gap between the skill levels I have, and that which I wish I had or know that I need?'

Thinking and talking about your intentions is a good start, but if you take a look in a dictionary or a thesaurus at the word 'practice', you will see something like this:

Practise (verb) to do repeatedly so as to gain skill
Practice (noun) something done regularly or habitually

(From the Oxford English Dictionary)

The thesaurus gives us these alternatives to the 'P' word:

Drill	Repeat
Exercise	Study
Go over	Train
Prepare	Pursue

As opposed to other 'P' words like: Procrastinate, Postpone and (pardon my language) Pissed off!!

If you want to make a lot of progress in a short time, you will need to think about when, where and how you practise. Whatever the skill you are aiming to improve, you will need a plan. You will also need to think about the circumstances and mindset with which you are going to practise. Are these going to help you to be focused and relaxed?

By managing the body as well as the mind we can have a positive impact on our rate of progress.

Getting started can feel like a slow and arduous task if you do it slowly, so my advice is to plan what you can do to make a difference and jump straight in!

Work in Progress
As I mentioned, there were many personal qualities that I had to work on in order to make the practise effective, namely:

Commitment	Self-belief
Persistence	Self-acknowledgement
Self-acceptance	Rewarding myself

I also looked hard at **where and how to practise**:

What conditions work?

And the strategy – target what specifically to work on:

> Tackle bite-sized chunks
>
> Measure what gets done
>
> Make it FUN!
>
> Celebrate success along the way

And most important of all: DISCIPLINE – not letting life get in the way!

Not all of you will be interested in how to practise and play a piano, but it is not only for those people that I write this book. The 'art of practising' follows the same format no matter what skill is being considered, so think laterally about what follows and ask yourself how you might use a similar idea and apply it to your own area of interest.

Your Tool Kit For Practice

> *Continuous effort – not strength or intelligence – is the key to unlocking our potential.*
>
> Winston Churchill

Commitment

Acknowledge that if it's a higher goal than you've reached for in the past, repeating what you have done before isn't enough to get you to where you want to go. You have to put in time and concentration on a regular basis to make it happen.

If half an hour a week is all you can manage, then you have to accept that you are dabbling, and not get angry with yourself that your ability is not improving very much.

My goal was to play the piano every day and to have a pre-determined amount that I was going to work on during each session.

Persistence

Reminding yourself that persistence will eventually pay off can help keep you focused on success when the going feels slow.

When the practice seemed tough or painful for me, I had only to think of the car crash and how lucky I was to be alive, to put it all into perspective. If I needed support beyond that, I would turn my thoughts down memory lane to when I first had piano lessons at school. Remembering my curiosity and determination to master what had at first seemed like an impossible task – making two hands play different things at different times, moving in opposite directions, with different timings to each – would remind me that I could achieve what had at first seemed impossible.

If you have followed my lead from Chapter 6 – Boost Your Belief – you will have already made a note about your personal memories that prove your talent in the areas of persistence and success. Having these at the front of your mind is ammunition for your success. Mental preparation in advance will mean that when you encounter obstacles, they are less likely to stop you moving forward.

Self-Acceptance

I had to accept where my technical abilities were, without judgement about how it should be, and be willing to start from there taking it one step at a time. There was always going to be a temptation to compare the lack of dexterity in my fixed, but once broken hand, to the skill that I remembered having as an eighteen-year-old.

Berating myself for not being as good as I once was, or for that matter being angry with myself for feeling fear once I started playing in front of other people, was a waste of time and energy. I found this out the hard way. Hindsight always has a more appropriate answer!

Could you be more accepting of yourself in order to make your progress less painful?

Self-Belief

I've devoted the whole of Chapter 6 to self-belief, so, by now, you should have gathered plenty of tools to help you with this. However, it's important to remember that this works in tandem with the other key skills that you'll need – commitment, persistence, self-acceptance, etc. Self-belief alone will get you started, but you need to combine it with these other skills to reach the goal that you strive for.

Self-Acknowledgement

As you make progress it's important to acknowledge and praise yourself.

Making a mental note, in my experience, doesn't last, and the temptation is to focus on how far you still have to go and bemoan the state of affairs. Have a book where you can chart your progress or even a grid on the wall that shows how much time and what specifically you have achieved so far. Give yourself a star each time you practise or reach a milestone in your plan. That negative voice in your head, which may have sounded loud and made you feel inadequate, has no room to move in the face of evidence to the contrary.

Encourage Praise and Support From Others

It is lovely when praise comes from those around you, but, ultimately, we need to acknowledge our own achievements and allow ourselves to feel good, no matter what other people are saying.

It makes a tremendous difference to know that someone notices the effort and dedication being put in. It costs nothing to share praise and provides an awful lot, not only for the person who receives it, but for the person who offers it too. If you give effective praise yourself, others will pick up the habit from you and hopefully some will come back your way.

However, not all people can read minds or notice what it is that makes a difference, so you may have to spell out what kind of verbal encouragement would help and support you – especially from those people closest to you. If you ask and it's not forthcoming, praise and reward yourself anyway.

Reward Yourself

You are much more likely to enjoy hard work if you know that you will be rewarded for it. Also, the enjoyment of a reward is that much sweeter when you know you have really earned it. There are things which you could add in along the way as you strive for your goal to reward the progress that you make.

Have a list to hand of all the things that you could include as rewards to tempt you with more vigour and enthusiasm towards your interim and final goal posts. Make the value of the reward comparable to the size and significance of your achievement. It might be a trip to a spa or lunch with a friend or a round on the golf course.

If there is no provision for time out and joyful events until you reach your end goal, it will make for a miserable time en route. Taking care of yourself will boost how you feel and will ultimately help you to arrive at your destination more sanely and quickly anyway, so build in the rewards from the start.

Patience

Sometimes all that is needed to make the transition to the next level of accomplishment is time and a good night's sleep.

At times I would find myself going over and over one section of music and not be able to make it flow, no matter how I broke it down or how slowly and meticulously I tried. I found that if

I could just leave it alone after I had done all the drilling, the next day it would miraculously feel so much easier.

It is an art in itself to trust that we have done all that we can and let the subconscious go to work while we are sleeping.

How and Where To Work

- Set the scene
- Admit what doesn't work
- Apply what does

Set The Scene

Even before I start to play the piano to practise, there are things that I can do which help me to concentrate. Knowing what I want the outcome to be, I set the scene, and focus my mind on the task.

To nurture a plant to grow to its best potential requires a certain amount of sunlight, water, food, and the right size pot for it to flourish. When you set the scene to practise, think of all the factors around you in terms of this plant and what conditions it will need to achieve the strongest growth. Your family could help to provide the right environment – the sunlight. Knowing what aspect of the task you are working on will provide the boundary and the pot. To help you make best use of your time, taking care of your mental and physical state before you begin is like pouring water on the plant.

My local hairdressers are great at setting the scene. When you have your hair washed, you are ushered into a small room with tea lights all lit and twinkling from the shelves, subtly reflected on the mirrored walls. Relaxing music is piped from speakers at each corner of the room, the subtle tones of yellow on the wall add to the tranquillity, the water is warm on your head, and the hairdresser's hands skilfully massage your scalp once the washing is over. You come out of that room feeling like a different person from the one that walked in. You can imagine how that has an impact on the experience for the customer and also the nature of the person the hairdresser gets to talk to whilst you are there.

Now suppose that you were able to access that relaxed, calm state of mind and take it to your practice. It will have a major, positive impact on your ability to concentrate. (As I write this there are children screaming in the background at the library – what irony!)

So ask yourself what could you do to most effectively set the scene for what you need to do?

Admit What Doesn't Work...
Have everything you need to hand, so you're not up and down for simple things like a pencil, a cup of tea, a jumper

because your back is cold ... (These came to my mind now, because they are what I think I need to go and get rather than continuing to write! OK, so I'm not perfect, I went to make the tea, and had a chocolate biscuit, and now I'm warmer with my jumper on!)

Relationships at home need special care when people are striving for different goals. When I was working towards the concerts, life at home was challenging. I was living with my husband again and our relationship was still not on solid ground. When I wanted to practise in the evenings after work, there would be times when we both wanted to use the lounge for different purposes. I would want to do some piano practise and he wanted to watch the TV. Not wanting to disturb him, I would try to do the practise with my head phones on to cut out the external sound from the digital piano. This did not work. I could hear the TV in the background and I would be thinking, 'Why can't he get dinner ready? He can see I have to practise.' When I asked him about this he would say that after a hard day at work, his watching TV was just as important as any piano practice I had to do. We disagreed many a time over this. It did not help me to concentrate, or help him to relax, nor help our relationship. It's easy now the time has passed to by sympathetic to both sides of that story, but at the time, such occasions were fraught with tension. Effective negotiation was not our strong spot.

There is a programme that I have discovered since starting to write this book that would have helped us to more effectively resolve such a scenario. The DVD and workbook set entitled, *The Art and Science of Love* by Dr John Gottman and Dr Julie Schwartz offers supportive, practical and constructive guidance for interpersonal relationship issues and comes highly recommended by me! You can find a link to them on my web site, or turn to the Resources section for their contact details.

Continue the conversation and negotiation so that both your needs feel met. Sort out a schedule so that each of you can achieve your respective goals – whatever they may be. You will need all the support you can get if you are truly pushing your boundaries. And there is no point going for such a goal if, in the mean time, the manner in which you achieve it alienates your nearest and dearest.

> *We should learn from the mistakes of others, we don't have time to make them all ourselves.*
>
> Groucho Marx

And What Does ...

Move To Where You Have Peace and Tranquillity

We had two reception rooms downstairs, but I was reluctant to move the piano to the other one, as we didn't have any heating there. Knowing that I really needed absolute concentration to be able to move forward, and to preserve my sanity, the piano was moved. I invested in a heater, and would still wear my headphones so I wouldn't be disturbed if the TV was on next door.

Turn Off The Phone

I love to receive phone calls from my friends and family, but taking calls in the middle of my practice would take away my concentration and use valuable practice time. When I got back to the piano keys my full attention wasn't there anymore, and I was less focused on my carefully pre-determined outcome. I learnt to turn the phone off, to actually turn my mobile off and unplug the landline. It was amazing the effect that this had on my concentration – when I knew that I wouldn't be interrupted.

Choose Carefully The Time Of Day

What is your most focused, productive and clear thinking time of the day?

Have you tried working at your task at different times of the day to see how the results might differ?

Although I had thought for years that I wasn't 'a morning person', I find that my mind is sharp and I can achieve more in a shorter time when I get up and work at 6am, so it's more efficient and effective to use my time in this way. Choose your time of practice with this knowledge in mind.

Put Practice First

If you work full time, then when you get home there will be many other things that could tempt your attention first, like putting the shopping away, opening the mail, listening to the answering machine messages, visiting the bathroom, getting the washing on, feeding the cat – the list could be endless. Turn off the phones and get on with it!

There are two schools of thought… if you know that you work better with all these things done first, then find a way to have them finished so that you still have the mental reserves to invest in the practice you need to do.

Be Smart About Where You Practise

Your living room is not the only place that you could choose to play a piano, rehearse or practise the skill you wish to improve. If you arrange to go to a church or a village hall to play a piano or practise a speech, there will be no distractions. With other skills you may find that the library or a special room in your house works better.

For me, variety in where I play makes a big difference, not only to my concentration, but also with getting used to playing in unfamiliar surroundings. Even with writing this book, the discipline of practice and giving it time has meant that I have had to be creative with my planning to keep me on track. I have moved house since I took on the piano challenge. My new home has a lounge and kitchen, which are open plan. I work on my laptop at the dining table. I am not always at my most focused working there with a view of the pots from breakfast, or being able to hear the washing machine at work.

Whilst writing this book, one of my most productive times was spent at my friend Mo's house. Mo is the professional speaker that you have heard about, with a passion and talent to impersonate Victoria Wood. She is also the person who set me the challenge to accompany her playing the piano.

I was able to combine work and play by writing at Mo's house. My productivity and focus was dramatically enhanced within the sanctuary of her office, and I had the joy of her company as a reward once I had finished. By being out of my own home I was removing distractions that might come from thinking about working on other things, and perhaps even more importantly, I felt supported by working there because she understands the need to concentrate when writing, as she is an accomplished author herself.

Where Do You Work/practise Your Skills?

Is there an alternative location that would afford you more concentration?

Work With Someone

Working alone may not be the easiest way to maintain momentum and enthusiasm. Knowing that someone else is working on a similar quest at the same time has been helpful, both with playing a piano and also with writing this book.

With the piano practice, I would sometimes call my girlfriend, Becky, (who also plays the piano) just before my practice session to tell her what I intended to work on. As she knew what I was talking about, I felt more accountable relating the information to her than to someone who didn't play. Also, by talking to her, it would remind me to put something into the practice session that would be fun for us to play when we were next together.

For the writing, besides working at Mo's house, I would work with Angela Sherman, whom I met at a networking event; she's a brilliant copywriter. We started talking and discovered we were both writing books. We set up calls where we would speak for ten minutes, get everything off our minds in a condensed fashion, say what we were going to work on for the next hour or so, and then both get to it. At the end of the agreed time we would speak again about what we had achieved. I found that during those sessions my concentration level was much higher than when I worked alone. Knowing that we were in it together, that I was being supported and that someone would want to hear what I had achieved when

I had finished, heightened my commitment to make progress. In this way, I was able to work at home some of the time.

Is there someone whom you might work with in a similar way?

The Strategy

Those who fail to plan, plan to fail!

Attempt Bite-Sized Chunks

Breaking the challenge into bite-sized chunks with a time frame, will help you to avoid feeling overwhelmed and defeated before you begin. Throwing yourself at the task without a plan may feel good in the beginning, as you will be doing a lot, but further down the track you may discover that the direction and pace may not be right. Following a planned route may be a more assured path to success.

I have to admit that planning is not one of my strengths. It's one of the limiting beliefs that I am still working on! I do know its value though, and I have seen the difference that it can make not only to my level of concentration and focus, but most importantly to my ability to rest and be kind to myself part way through a project. When I can see evidence on paper that I am on track, and when I also have on paper the next steps that I need to take, I sleep better and feel a lot more confident and assured in reaching my goal. Without the plan, common consequences for me are living with a constant fretful feeling about not having done enough, and sometimes waking in the middle of the night.

It can be an art in itself to learn how to gauge your time and be realistic about what you can achieve in an hour, week or month with regard to your plan. Having interim milestones to aim for, as well as daily action plans, will make things much more manageable.

Know and record on paper what you want to achieve at each session

Overestimating what you can achieve in a certain time can mean that your lists never get completed. So notice how often you set the target and fall short.

Did You Achieve What You Set Out to Achieve Today?
If not, how far behind your target were you by the end of the session?

See if you can re-jig your plan to take account of what you learn by asking these questions.

I am not a fan of realistic goals all the time – I think it's good to dream and reach for the stars. However, even I have to admit that my page-long 'To Do' lists just leave me exhausted before I start, knowing that there's no way I can get it all done.

One technique that I have used successfully is to only have the three most pertinent things that I want to achieve on the list in front of me. As each one is achieved, I put a highlighter mark over it and move onto the next. When all three are completed, only then do I give my attention to what else needs doing. That way, I am not likely to be distracted by things that may seem easier to do, but which are less important that my main focus for the day.

Measure What Gets Done

> *What gets measured gets done!*   Henry Mintzberg

When practising the piano, you need to have an objective even if it is as small as to learn a few notes, playing with one hand at a time. If you go back over it the next day and link it to the next few notes, your progress is assured! You can apply this to any skill you are planning to learn.

Relying on your mind to tell you how much progress you have made is not the best way to stay positive. Human beings have a tendency to focus on that which still has to be done. Have a book that details your daily practice goals. It's a good motivator and great boost to the confidence to look back to see just how far you've come. Each day before you start your 'practice', make a note of the answers to these questions:

1. What specifically am I working on today?
   e.g., for the piano, which line of the music? At what speed? What do I want to improve – The tone? The speed? The level of emotion?
   e.g., for writing the book, which chapter am I working on? What do I want the reader to do as a result of reading it?

2. What do I want the outcome of the session to be?

Relevant no matter what the subject!

Having to answer the question, 'What, specifically, am I working on?', keeps me away from the temptation to want to play the whole piece of music when I practise. My undisciplined self can be like a kid in a sweet shop, wanting to try a little of everything rather than being willing to settle for the flavour of just one sweet. I am not suggesting that you must only work on one thing at a time; we do need a mental break and a bit of variety to maintain interest and enthusiasm.

We all reach a point of saturation, having worked on the same thing for a length of time. Being willing to leave it alone and trust that you have made progress is another skill to practise. The following day you will be rewarded with evidence of that. In the words of an inspiring speaker by the name of Nigel Risner,

We are after progress not perfection!

Having one piece of music on the piano stand at a time, helps to narrow my focus. Often I have three pieces on the go, but if all of them are in front of me at once, then I will always be thinking ahead. The same applies if I have clutter on my desk when I am writing. My neighbour, Jim, reminded me that every piece of paper that you have yet to deal with occupies a small piece in your mind.

How much of your mind is already engaged elsewhere and not available for the task at hand? Clearing up unfinished business or moving it aside, knowing that it will get dealt with later, leaves more mental space to work with.

The value of having somewhere to note your progress and make a record of what you want to achieve has been mentioned before. I mention it again, as this is the ideal point to put it into practise. It will help to focus your mind and be a great record of how far you've come (and when you are writing your own book about how you did it, it will serve as a great reminder of how you got there!)

Prepare Your Mind

If you are going to put in the practice once you get home from work, apply your mind to the task before you get there and think about it whilst travelling home. Your mind will be more focused and ready for action when you arrive, if you have mentally prepared and thought through your actions. Think about what it is that you want to achieve.

Steve McDermott has written a book called, *How to Be a Complete and Utter Failure in Life, Work and Everything – 39 Ways to Lasting Underachievement*. This is a motivational book in reverse, and talks about the importance of getting into 'the right state', rather than getting in 'a right state.'

If I lack focus because of events whirling in my mind, I will listen to a soothing classical recording to calm me down. If my energy levels are low, to inject some adrenalin into my system, I'll take a quick walk up the street or even get out my skipping rope and skip on the drive. Failing that, I will listen to some up-beat dance music before I begin.

Enlisting the help of people around you can help in many ways too. For example, if they are willing to take care of other things that you might otherwise have your mind on, like walking the dog, or putting the washing on, it removes one more thing that your brain might otherwise be occupied by. This way you free up your brain space for your practice.

Without this kind of preparation your amount of attention may resemble something like this:

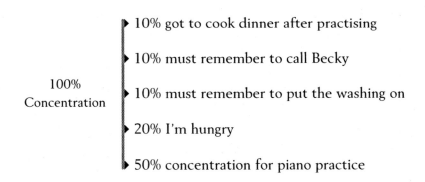

More information about state management to help get that last figure up from 50% to nearer 100% can be found in the chapter that follows about fear and managing the symptoms that it generates.

After focusing my mind, I wake up the tactile senses in my fingers by going through simple scales and warm-up patterns up and down the keyboard.

Starting with a repetitive exercise going up and down the notes allows each finger to make contact with the keys, helps me shift my mental attention from what has been going on before I play, and gets the muscles in my fingers ready for action. The accuracy needed to play is not only about hitting the right notes, but also about how hard I press the keys, so I have to tune-in to the sensation from my fingertips. As I type now, and think about this, I am more aware of the resistance from each letter on the keyboard.

You may be thinking this is not relevant unless you play a piano or type, but there is an equivalent here for you. What's your strategy to warm up the muscles that you need for effective practice? Think about your strategy!

Have Some Fun!

With the daily drill of practice it is easy to lose the fun element. If you write on your plan what you are going to do for fun today, then you will have something to look forward to rather than just seeing the chore.

When I am being kind to myself and taking a dose of my own medicine, at the end of a practise session, I will put one of the backing tracks on my digital piano and cross something like Jingle Bells with a heavy rock beat, or I will work on an easy piece that I know I will get to play as a duet with Becky the next time I see her. This addition lightens my mind and shifts my thinking from discipline to fun.

As you reach a significant milestone in your plan, don't forget to take one of those rewards that you have planned for yourself!

What can you do for fun at the end of a practice session?

What rewards for progress will you build into your plan?

Never grow a wish bone where your back bone ought to be.

Clementine Paddleford

Dealing With Frustrations

There will be many 'perfect' reasons that could stand in the way of your time and your mental focus. Discipline is what will allow you to practise even when you don't feel like it.

If you get into the habit of practice you'll sustain growth. Without it, what you have will dwindle away. When I first had some lessons in juggling, this point was really highlighted for me. Although I would apply plenty of time and effort to the art of practising juggling with my three small beanbags one day, if I did not touch them again for a week, then the progress that I had made went back to zero!

Taking up a new skill means that you have to learn the art of being a beginner again remembering the importance of regular commitment, dedication and willingness to not expect perfection straight away.

It's Like Brushing Your Teeth ...

As a youngster I am sure there were times when you screamed because you didn't want to brush your teeth, but your parents, wanting the best for you, got you to do it anyway. This habit became a routine that hopefully will have preserved your teeth for much longer than they would otherwise have been around.

If you are able to step over your reasons like: too tired; not in the mood; want to watch something on TV – it will help you to re-affirm your commitment and put you in charge of your feelings rather than at the mercy of them. Getting into the habit while things are going well, will give you more resilience to keep making progress when the going gets tough.

When I was practising for the concerts, life at home was difficult. My marriage was not at its best. There was a lot of conflict and many times that I was upset when I thought there was no point sitting down to practise because it wouldn't make a difference. Having a deadline in the form of a concert looming, meant that I couldn't allow the emotion to get in the way.

One of the most useful exercises that I used on many occasions, was to notice how I was feeling, really identify what was going on, and then to step aside from that, as if I were another person observing myself. I would practise switching from one perspective to the other and back again, so that although the feelings were there, they no longer dictated my actions.

Exercise[1] – Changing Your Perception
Knowing that you can change your perception and your perspective to put unhelpful feelings on hold is a powerful tool to have in your kit bag. Practising these techniques will increase your ability to concentrate in many areas or your life. Apply this technique when you need to focus your attention, or when you feel under pressure.

Be aware of your posture. Sit up tall and breathe deeply such that you notice your abdomen moving in and out.

Step 1 – As you sit quietly, tune into your emotions. Be fully aware of the feelings that you have. Ask yourself what specifically is it that you feel? Anger, frustration, hurt? Notice where in your body you can feel it. Take a few seconds to identify this.

Step 2 – Now imagine that you have the ability to step outside your body so that you can look back at yourself. Imagine that you are sitting in a different chair and watching yourself. In your mind you are looking at a different person and you are no

---

[1]. An audio programme is available from my web site that will guide you through the exercises listed above and in subsequent chapters of the book. Once you have listened to this a few times you will find that you are able to make use of the skill without an audio prompt. www.tracyplaice.com/FTMAW/audio

longer influenced by any of those feelings. It is as though you are observing someone else with them.

Step 3 – Now switch your perception back again to your initial position, again aware of those initial feelings. Notice that the impact of the feeling has reduced and does not seem so acute.

Step 4 – In your mind, make a mental move again, back to the alternative chair and observe yourself.

Notice how different you feel in each of these positions and practise switching perspectives until the feelings that were bothering you, no longer have the same intensity.

Engrossed in the practice, my mind would be able to rest. Afterwards, I felt peaceful and proud to have got beyond the reasons and practised anyway. The feeling is akin to that which is available through guided meditation, which I was introduced to during my time in Australia.

Chart Your Progress

Once you have finished your practice session, record your progress. As I suggested earlier in this chapter, recording your achievements as you go along will help you to maintain proof that you are on track and bring you peace of mind about your rate of progress. There remains a little child in all of us who likes to be rewarded and praised. I believe you are never too old to appreciate gold stars on a chart to show the world your achievement!

Expert Opinion

One of the experts that I consulted about this chapter is Dominic Alldis, who is Head of the Jazz Department at the Royal College of Music. His comments were that in his view, practice should always be fun, and that if one day he sat down to play and it wasn't fun, then he would leave it alone and go and do something else instead. In this way, he said, whenever you sit down to play, you will associate it with a positive experience that you want to repeat.

What's the piano in your life?
Whatever skill you might be working on, ask yourself what conditions and strategies will help you to make the best progress. Apply your mind to the task before you get there and then follow your predetermined plan. Know specifically what you want the outcome to be and, when you achieve this, stop, take a break, and reward yourself!

Summary

• Choose your most productive time.

• Work with someone.

• Delegate tasks that free your mind from responsibility.

Say No to: Phone calls in the middle of practice.

TV on in the background.

More than one 'piece of music' on the stand at a time (or more than one task to focus on in front of you).

And Yes to: S et the scene

S low your brain waves

S elect your objective

H one your concentration

H ave fun

H onour your progress

8 | Dealing with Symptoms of Fear

The only thing we have to fear is fear itself.'

President Franklin D. Roosevelt

Feeling the Fear

When you are making changes to your life that push you beyond your comfort zone, not only will you be forcing your mind to go somewhere uncomfortable, but you will be pushing your body too. The connection between your mind and your body is stronger than you think. Even in the face of a fantastically rehearsed plan, your subconscious mind can interfere and trigger reactions in your body, such as:

✓ Churning stomach   ✓ Irritable bowels

✓ Confused mind   ✓ Sweaty palms

✓ Twitching eyelids   ✓ Knocking knees

✓ Headaches   ✓ Being too hot

✓ Feelings of agitation ✓ Being too cold

The symptoms alone can make you start to shake, feel anxious and become confused. We've all felt such feelings for many different reasons, although we all react to them in different ways. What's at stake, and the amount of worry and anxiety that you are carrying about the event, will determine the extent to which these symptoms get to you!

When I first took steps to play a piano for other people, the feelings that I experienced were akin to riding a roller coaster. As I approached the instrument, it was like walking up to the carriage. I knew that once I was in my seat, I would be locked in place, would slowly climb to the top, the muscles in my stomach tightening in anticipation, highly aware that any second now, my stomach would be left at the top of the slope as my body plummeted to the bottom. Once I began, there was no going back, so I just had to give in to whatever happened next. It might work out or I might make a mistake, or my brain might totally disengage and leave me frozen to the spot.

Those people who are able to react well to symptoms of fear have an opportunity to allow their ability to shine. Those who don't learn how to overcome them, may never know what talent lies waiting, hidden beneath the surface.

Not being aware that you can do something about these physical symptoms is what causes many people to quit. Even the famous and revered can feel stage fright. I heard recently on Radio 4 that the opera singer, Renee Flemming, battled with extreme stage fright for two years at University. In fact, she nearly quit because of it. Similarly, in Billy Connolly's biography, *Billy*, we learn that his pre-performance nerves are so bad that Pamela Stephenson, his wife and author of the book, always wonders whether he will pull it off.

Classic FM Magazine ran a story written by Julian Haylock about the life of the composer Chopin, who, he said, was 'driven to paroxysms of blind terror in front of a large audience'. In Chopin's own words, 'I feel asphyxiated by its eager breath, paralysed by its inquisitive stare, silenced by its alien faces'. Chopin retired from the platform in 1832, having made only 30 concert appearances in his entire career.

As a population we seem to have a weird fascination with watching people face a fear. You only have to consider the number of reality shows that proliferate on the television these days to recognise this. See how popular shows like *Faking It* and *I'm a Celebrity, Get Me Out of Here* are, and you will get my point.

Ironic, isn't it, how so many of us are perfectly happy to watch others face and conquer their fears, yet are less ready to question what we might have to gain from facing a fear ourselves?

It was education and repeated exposure to the symptoms that allowed me to gradually change my physical responses and, eventually, to play a piano confidently in front of others. By increasing my knowledge about how fear affects the body and the mind and by using several techniques that encompassed how I thought, what I ate, how I took care of myself and how I approached a once-fearful scenario, I was able to counteract those potentially debilitating effects.

If you understand what happens to your body and mind when you feel fear, it can help you to find a way to do something about it. What follows will not make those feelings go away completely, but will give you plenty of ideas about how to minimise them in order to use the kick of adrenalin produced to your best advantage. This knowledge will put you in control, rather than at the mercy of your nerves.

Those of you who wish to continue with the story rather than read about theory may wish to skip forward to chapter 9 and come back to this one later. Those of you who are preparing for a scenario which will put you in the public eye, and in need of help to control nerves, should read on.

> *Top athletes who are best able to harness the power of adrenalin win gold medals.*
> Don Greene, sports psychologist and author of *Fight Your Fear and Win*

A Chemistry and Anatomy Lesson

The outward symptoms of fear are the end result of changes that take place in the body, stimulated by chemical changes in the brain. The symptoms of fear can be put into three categories:

- Physical   • Mental   • Behavioural

Physical Changes

An event that prompts a feeling of fear starts with a response from an area of the brain called the hippocampus. This causes a gland called the hypothalamus to initiate adrenalin to be released from the adrenal medulla of the adrenal glands which sit just above the kidneys. This triggers a number of responses over which we have no control. These responses include:

✓ Adrenalin flooding into the bloodstream

✓ Increased heart rate

✓ Rapid, shallow breathing, dilation of the bronchioles in the lungs allowing greater ventilation.

✓ Vision narrowing to a central spot causing us to become less aware of our peripheral vision.

✓ Increased blood flow to the large muscles in readiness to take flight from our perceived aggressor.

To protect itself from injury, your body reacts by restricting the amount of blood available for the major organs. Instead, the blood is sent to your larger muscles so you are ready to run away. You'll find your hands are cold and your hand-eye-brain co-ordination is not as good as usual. You may feel a bit distracted, as though you have lost some of your connections, which can make you feel a bit disorientated.

Physical changes that happen to the body as a result of feeling fear also cause a chemical reaction that prompts feelings of anxiety. When you feel anxious, sugar levels are used up at a much faster rate than normal; hence, the blood sugar level in the body can plummet with worry. As the sugar level drops you feel hungry and may feel a bit faint. Your body may respond by releasing stored sugar, or you may naturally respond to the hunger symptom by eating something that will give you a 'quick fix', like chocolate and biscuits. As your sugar level comes back up again, it gets burnt off and again plummets, continuing the yo-yo effect on your system. This can have a negative impact on a number of areas:

The Immune System

A chemical called cortisol is a by-product of worry. This chemical reduces the effectiveness of macrophage cells, whose job it is to digest the debris of dead cells in the blood and bring infection fighting cells to the region. So if the macrophages don't work properly, the immune system doesn't work properly either.

Digestion

In a state of worry, automatic responses divert available blood supply away from areas like the stomach and bowels to the heart, lungs, brain and larger muscles to enable us to be ready to take flight and run. As a consequence of resources being diverted, food that remains in the bowels either rushes through the system or becomes stagnant. So when it passes through quickly, you get 'the runs' – hence the phrase (and please pardon my language) 'shit scared' – and when the process slows down, you end up with constipation.

Sleep Patterns

When you are worrying about an approaching event as you try to go to sleep, there will be excess adrenalin coursing through your veins. As adrenalin is the product that provides impetus and stimulation, is it any wonder that you can't sleep?!

In the face of all the above, it is not surprising that you would rather avoid the situation.

Mental Effects

While fear can increase your mental alertness, helping you to cope with a scary scenario, it can also trigger your instinct to try to avoid the danger and focus on how to get away from the situation – fast! This is one of the reasons why, when you are scared, you may find yourself rushing a performance in order to get it over with.

At the onset of anxiety, your left-brain, that's the side of the brain that handles the logical and practical functions, goes cı ızy. It takes one look at the situation in which you find yourself, such as on a stage in front of 300 people without having rehearsed and says, 'No way, José!'

From that moment all your left-brain sees is the negative aspects of that situation, all the things that could go wrong and the potential failure. Your mind affects your body, which in turn affects your mind; after all, if your knees are knocking, you must be really frightened, right? Our mental reaction effectively perpetuates the physical one in a vicious feedback loop.

Because of the opposite reactions from the left and right brain, it can feel like there is a war going on in our heads when faced with fearful situations. We need to shift our thinking and allow the knowledge and wisdom contained in the right side of the brain to take over, so that we can perform at our best. The left and right side of the brain have different roles to play:

Left Brain	Right Brain
The analytical side.	The creative side – has positive thoughts and the wealth of wisdom
In the face of fear, this part of the brain notices the symptoms of fear and instils a sense of panic.	Will allow you to perform at your peak if not interfered with too much by limiting thoughts from the left side of the brain.
Gets busy analysing, criticizing and distracting you. It turns your fears into obsessions and impels you to get out of the situation as fast as you can.	In the face of fear and nervous feelings, this is the place from which you draw on your instinct, training and muscle memory.

I've watched many a cartoon where the emotion of fear is portrayed with a character sweating, shivering, and knees knocking. I had always seen that as a comical exaggeration. I was very surprised to experience the last feature for myself when at the age of fifteen, I gave a presentation from a pulpit to a massive audience in Holland. This was my first trip away from home to Europe. As I mentioned before, I was a member of a Ukrainian folk dance group, led by my maths teacher, Mr Czuplak. We were there to take part in the annual folk festival.

I can still vividly picture myself standing there, high up on the carved, wooden pulpit, wearing my blue and red velvet

Ukrainian costume. With flowers on my head and ribbons hanging by my side, the Bible poised in my hands, and 300 pairs of eyes staring up, waiting for me to begin.

I looked the part, but inside I felt completely lost; my mouth felt dry as a bone, and I cursed myself for being so eager to please and opening my mouth before I'd considered the implications.

It was typical of me, speaking before my brain engaged. I'd volunteered to represent our group and read the lesson in Amsterdam Cathedral, the morning after our performance. Like an idiot I had only practised once. I had read through the script to a friend, who had just advised me to slow down a bit.

As I began to read, I kept telling myself to go slowly. I refused to let fear take a complete hold of me, but it was a really strange sensation as I became aware of my knees knocking beneath me.

I was told after the event that I had read the passage really well. They complimented me on how calm and confident I appeared. I was SO glad that the skirt I was wearing was long enough to cover the evidence that would have proved otherwise.

It is only once you have been through such a scenario, that you get to prove to yourself that it is possible to cover the evidence of fear. Believing that people can sense your fear can make you anxious; it can diminish your confidence and self-esteem and, ultimately, your performance. Calling on previous examples of where you have been able to 'fake it' will counteract that potential limitation. If you have no examples of this, then putting into practise what you learn from the next chapter will provide you with plenty!

Behavioural Effects

Fear affects your behaviour too, as you become unable to do things that would normally come naturally. For example, when you are frightened of giving a presentation at work, you end up not giving yourself enough time to prepare, falsely believing that it won't make any difference to practise, with accompanying thoughts like, 'It's going to be a disaster anyway.'

If you can rationalise that these are the normal symptoms of nerves, you can placate the mind long enough for you to consider what actions you can take, and then go and do something about them!

Reframing

The same symptoms that signal fear in the body, are also the same as those we experience when we feel excited. So the first method of counteracting the impact of the symptoms of fear is to tell yourself, once they start, that this means that you are excited. In NLP this is known as re-framing.

Deepen Your Breathing

One of the first physical symptoms to change when stressed is your breathing. The physical symptoms are less likely to escalate if you are aware and counteract it straight away with slower, more deliberate breathes.

After my first public piano performance at a concert, I remember vividly the relief that I felt as I sat down in my seat and breathed out. I wondered if I had actually held my breath for the whole performance. Given that it was a major event with major stresses, it is not really a surprise that this happened, however, in future performances, I made sure I tackled this aspect.

Correct breathing is vital in the campaign to minimise the effects of fear on the body. With a reduced amount of oxygen available to your brain, your ability to concentrate and perform at your best is bound to be diminished. The most effective method of breathing which provides the most calming effect, involves taking air in slowly and deeply, so that you feel it down in the region of your stomach. Most of the time we breathe in a very shallow way, with the breath reaching only the very top of our chest, barely filling our lungs with air.

Try to become aware of your breathing. Stand up taller, sit up straighter, and give yourself a few moments several times a day to breathe deeply and effectively. This will keep the grey matter ticking over at its best, and heighten your awareness about the state of your posture as well as your intake of air.

An Exercise to 'Psych-Down' and Focus The Mind

By focusing on external stimuli that you can see, hear and feel, this exercise helps to distract your attention from your thoughts and into the present moment to aid your concentration and focus.

(My thanks to Andy Clarke of AC Pro Speaker for teaching me this technique before one of my performances.)

The exercise has seven steps and will take you 5-10 minutes to do the first few times, but with practice you will be able to access a focused mental state in a couple of seconds. As with any skill though, practice is the key to mastery.

This exercise can be done almost anywhere, although I suggest you avoid doing this while you are driving. You might be on the train, sitting in the armchair at home, or sitting at your desk.

Step 1 – Focus on How Your Body Feels

Start off by becoming aware of how your body feels. Think about where you find the weight in your body, your head, your shoulders or your legs, are they heavy, or relaxed? Become aware of the tension in your body. Choose three areas to focus on, and, in turn tense up each area, hold it for five seconds and then release it, maintaining your focus in that area for another couple of seconds before moving on. For example, tense up your hands, then release. Tense up your shoulders for five seconds and then release. Tense up your calf muscles, and then release.

Step 2 – Focus Your Vision

Now shift your focus from your body to look at what you can see directly ahead of you. First look at the broad picture, being aware of the whole picture, taking in your peripheral as well as your central vision. Then narrow your focus and pick three things from the central area to focus your attention on in turn. For example, if you are in your office, you might focus on the catch on the window frame for five seconds, then turn your attention to the plant on the window ledge for five seconds, then to the top of the calendar on the wall.

Step 3 – Focus Your Hearing

Now shift your attention to what you can hear. Pick out three separate sounds around you. Again with the office as an example, pay attention to the noise from your computer for five seconds, then be aware of the noise from the heating system for another five seconds, now turn your attention to the faint sound of the cars outside your office window, again for five seconds.

Step 4 – Back to Your Feelings

Leave your thoughts about vision and hearing behind and again become aware of how you feel. Choose the two areas from step one that felt most tense and, again, tense one area at a time, and release, this time for three seconds.

Step 5 – Back to Your Eyes

Choose two of the items previously concentrated on and give each of them three seconds of your attention.

Step 6 – Back to Your Hearing

Pick out just two sounds that you listened to before, pay attention to each of them in turn for only three seconds this time.

Step 7 – Now Just One Stimulus From Each Category

Pick just one area of your body, notice how it feels for a second, choose one visual aspect, look at that for a second, then pay attention to just one of the sounds for a second.

By now, your breathing will have become longer and deeper. You will be able to think calmly, and focus on the task at hand.

With practice you will be able to access this calm state by choosing to put your attention for one second to a feeling, a sight and then a sound to access that same calm mental state.

Count to Ten!

Many of you will be familiar with the saying 'Count to ten!' It is often said by people trying not to vent their anger and frustration. By putting your feelings on hold as you concentrate on counting the numbers, your mind is momentarily distracted and so the impact of the feeling is reduced. This allows you to choose how you act, rather than just react. The next time you come across a situation in which you know your body is providing you with evidence of fear and you know it is not going to help you, give this technique a try.

It's not that we don't know about many of these methods, just that we often forget to use them!

Expert Opinion

I consulted a number of professionals about the subjects covered in this book in order to bring you a broader perspective than my own. One of those people was Henry Hopking who is an expert in the field of maximising potential through effective use of brainpower. He uses this knowledge across many disciplines, especially with top golfing professionals, to help them access their best possible performance when it really counts.

Henry said that more of our mental capacity is available to use when we are calm and the brainwaves are slower, compared to when we are pumped up and excitable with faster brain patterns going on. More often than not, he said, he teaches clients techniques that help them to psych down, rather than psych up, in order to access their peak performance.

Since learning about this I have changed my preparation strategy en route to speaking engagements. At the beginning of the journey, I will play music that gives me a boost of energy and adrenalin – if I think I need it, but nearer the venue, as I go through my mental rehearsal of the performance, I will listen to music that has a calming effect rather than a rousing one. I have noticed that it does allow me to think more clearly.

The only way for you to find out what works for you is to experiment with these techniques. Let me know what you find and what difference it makes!

The amount of concern you have will be linked to the importance of the event, what is at stake and how worried you are about the scenario. The level at which you are able to perform is very well illustrated by Octavius Black and Sebastian Bailey in their book, *The Mind Gym*:

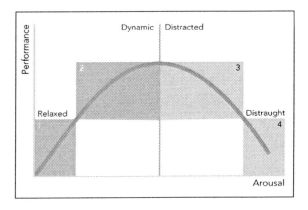

Through practice you can become used to the situation that makes you feel fear and be able to act beyond the physical symptoms that it may bring. The intention is to move the curve in the diagram to the right, so that you are confidently performing in Zone 2, rather than in Zone 3 or 4, you will then bring a once-distracted and distraught set of scenarios under the banner of 'feeling dynamic'. You'll find out more about how to do that in Chapter 9, Stepping Beyond the Comfort Zone.

Other Ways to Impact Your Feelings

Focus on the Outcome

You can use this technique in many situations, whether you are practising for a musical performance, working on a critical report for presentation, or in any other situation that you might need a high level of concentration and ability to be heard at your best.

When I was learning presentation skills with Toastmasters, we were taught to focus on the outcome that we wanted for our audience, rather than thinking about the exact words we had rehearsed. I found it quite easy to adopt this state of mind for presentations, but was not as strong at it when I had to play the piano for people. Not for want of trying though!

With a piano performance, I would concentrate on wanting to share the joy that I personally derived from the piece of music that I was about to play. If doubt crept in, my thoughts turned to hoping that I would get the notes right and avoid making a mistake, but I knew I had to practise focusing on something other than that to be able to perform at my best. It took a few concerts to be able to get this to work for me.

Don't expect to be able to get everything right in the beginning. With repetition things will improve but you have to be prepared to take a risk and put yourself outside your comfort zone to provide the opportunity to try it. That is the only way for you to find out if it works!

Visualise Success

Rehearse your performance in your mind. See yourself walking on stage (or wherever it is that you need to be) standing tall, smiling, feeling relaxed, looking at your best, and see yourself successfully completing the task. Imagine how you will feel as it all goes really well. By getting your brain used to those positive sensations, you will be creating a recognised pathway that will make this outcome more likely once you have rehearsed it. I still use this technique every time I prepare for a concert or speaking engagement.

Hypnotherapy

Sometimes people need professional help to move beyond a limiting belief or to change a physical reaction to stressful situations. Qualified hypnotherapists can help to unblock thoughts that come from the subconscious which prevent you from making the changes that you want, as mentioned briefly in Chapter 6.

Through relaxation methods, hypnotherapists can help you to create a more positive potential outcome for events which give you cause for concern and elicit feelings of fear. They do not put you in a trance and take control of your brain. Their techniques help you to relax and distract the conscious part of your mind so that change can take place at the subconscious level.

My friend and colleague Keith Banfield is an expert in this field. He helped me to revisit the time when I played the piano in front of my family as a youngster and froze. There are decisions that we make at crucial times in our childhood that have limiting effects on our beliefs about our abilities. By revisiting the scenario under his guidance I was able to put it in perspective.

That sounds simple enough and my rational mind would do this anyway, however, the impact of the subconscious is very strong and even with a well-rehearsed plan and action steps to progressively take me outside my comfort zone, there was still a deep association that I had of performing being a very unpleasant experience. Working with Keith helped me to create a more positive association.

Affirmations

What you say to yourself has a huge impact on the way that you perform. We are good at the phrases that say, 'I hope I don't mess it up' or, 'this is bound to be awful' but we are far less naturally disciplined at providing positive language that spurs us on and implies belief in our abilities.

Having a phrase that you repeat to yourself in your mind can help to support rather than undermine your efforts. Choose something as simple as 'You can do it!' or, 'You know you can do this!' Repeat often and eventually you will believe it!

How Food Can Help

As I stretched my comfort zone by giving presentations and playing a piano in public, my metabolism went a bit hay wire. Just before a concert I would feel ravenous sometimes, and sick at others; be constipated one day and then have the runs the next; be able to concentrate and then find my mind wandering all over the place. My body would burn calories at a much faster rate under this kind of pressure.

My degree in Optometry covered a fair bit about metabolism, but I wanted to know more about its control to help stop me being distracted by feeling like I was living on the end of a yo-yo.

To keep my mind and body in the best shape possible at these events, I would have to pay special attention to what food I ate in the lead-up. Firstly to avoid getting 'the runs' and secondly to keep my sugar level more stable. I read a lot about this and the most useful texts that I found are listed in the resource section. What appears below is a snippet of that information, but it will give you a glimpse of what might help.

According to Patrick Holford, author of *The Optimum Nutrition Bible*, managing your blood sugar level is the most important factor in maintaining even energy levels.

Situations that stress your mind and body cause more sugar and calories to be used. You can alter your food intake to try to counteract this effect, not just by eating more, but by knowing what type of foodstuffs help to keep your blood sugar levels on a more even keel.

In much the same way that a marathon runner will plan his fuel intake to obtain maximum output, and a diabetic person must be aware of their glucose level (the energy source most used by the body), you can use this knowledge to even out the physical responses when facing your own challenges.

Before performing it is better to eat complex carbohydrates in your meal to provide you with a stable and sustainable re-lease of energy. As the glucose in these food items is locked into larger molecules, they release it more slowly thus avoid-ing strong energy swings. Examples include potatoes, lentils, vegetables, brown rice, pasta, bread, oatmeal, beans, and fruit. As opposed to sugary foodstuffs such as those found in sweets, soft drinks, and ice cream. (This is a huge subject area and this is just a sample of a few things to consider. For more detailed information, consult the resources mentioned in this chapter.).

Many of us reach for food when we are frightened. Chocolate is one of our favourite 'soothers.' Probably a habit that has grown with us since childhood when we were given treats by our parents in order to make something better. Chocolate falls into a category of high glycaemic foods, which also includes biscuits and other sweets. They inject sugar into your blood-stream giving you a temporary high, which is the outcome you wanted to satisfy the hunger symptoms. Unfortunately as your sugar level plummets, you can feel worse than before. Foodstuffs like this are used by the body at a faster rate and actually amplify the up and down swing of symptoms related to varying blood sugar levels.

Interesting fact – Glenn Hoddle banned baked beans from the England football team's diet purely because of its sugar content.

Rosemary Stanton, nutritionist and author of *Eating for Peak Performance* makes the following recommendations about eating before an important event:

1. Eat 2-3 hours before the performance

2. Drink plenty of fluid, preferably water

3. Include complex carbohydrates in the meal such as cereals, wholemeal bread, muffins, rice, pasta, vegetables, especially potatoes or fruit

4. Avoid foods high in proteins and fats (red meat) as these take longer to digest

5. Eat foods that are familiar and enjoyable to you

6. Avoid large quantities of sugary foods because this gives you uneven bursts of energy

The body processes raw food much more easily than when it is cooked.

Vera Pfeiffer, author of *Positively Fearless*, suggests: 'Eat small portions of food at regular intervals to avoid varying sugar levels. Refined and processed foods make our bodies work harder. When you additionally suffer from anxiety or fear your biochemical processes are knocked off balance even further.'

Here are some other useful resources from nature's store cupboard that can help support us when we are stepping outside of our comfort zone.

Water

This comes top of the list. Drink more of it. We need to drink at least two litres of still water a day to maintain good hydration levels. Fizzy drinks and squashes do not count; neither do tea and coffee, though herbal teas are fine.

You will be burning more sugar as the fear factor kicks in. As the sugar is used up, water is used up too. If the body can't get it through a natural intake of water, it will draw water away from other cells in your body leaving you with potential symptoms from dehydration such as a dry tongue and a headache.

Ginger

Ginger settles the stomach and sailors used to swear by it on long voyages. I like to use it in fresh juice in the morning. I use a juicing machine and put fresh ginger with carrot, apple and celery. This is a great immune-boosting combination. Ginger can also be grated to add to stir-fry meals. Or start the day with a slice of fresh lemon and a slice of fresh ginger in hot water.

Celery

Celery stabilises sugar levels in the blood, so snack on this rather than chocolate.

Apricots and Dates

Dried apricots and dates offer a slow and sustained release of natural sugar for the body, which can give you the same initial buzz and satisfaction as chocolate, but without the rapid climb down. I snack on these with pumpkin seeds and cashew nuts when I know it is important to sustain my sugar levels.

Vitamin B complex

Dr Roland author of *The Confident Performer* reminds us that when we are under the stress of performing, the body has increased metabolic needs. This increase requires more B complex vitamins and increases protein use which, in turn, requires more calcium in the diet.

The range of B vitamins are known to help the nervous system to function properly. As they are water soluble, you will not overdose on these vitamins, but you must remember to drink enough water to be able to absorb them.

B and C vitamins are vital for turning food into mental and physical energy. They are richest in fresh fruit and vegetables.

Vitamin C

Vitamin C enhances the immune system, protects you from in.ections and colds, promotes healing after illness and injury and also helps the adrenal glands to function properly. When you are under stress your adrenal glands have to work harder than ever, so this vitamin is particularly important. Any citrus fruit is a great source of vitamin C.

Although my diet is normally rich in fresh fruit and vegetables, when I was really pushing my boundaries and starting to perform in concerts, I took supplements to boost my levels of vitamin B and C to be sure that I had all that I needed. It was easier for me to take a tablet than to add up what amount I would get from certain foods. I'm not suggesting that this is the best way, but I want you to be aware of how factors such as this can be worked into your plan.

Calcium and Magnesium

Both of these minerals have a soothing effect on the nervous system and are natural tranquillisers. Always take these two together as they enhance each other's absorption. If you lack calcium you feel nervous and on edge. Bran blocks absorption of calcium, so if you eat a lot of bran, you should add calcium to your diet. Calcium is found in large quantities in dairy produce.

Zinc

Zinc has a positive influence on cell growth and resistance to infection. It is involved in hormone production and good mental function. It also has a stabilising effect on the central nervous system and is prescribed as a counterbalance to anxiety. Watch out though – zinc absorption is blocked by tea, coffee, and alcohol.

All 'seed' foods which include nuts, lentils, dried beans, as well as peas, broad beans, runner beans and whole grains – are good sources of zinc.

Tea and Coffee

Try to avoid drinking coffee and tea as they are diuretics, which means that they cause you to eliminate more water than you take in by drinking them. Also the caffeine within them is a stimulant which creates physiological effects similar to adrenalin. When you are about to perform, you probably have more than enough adrenalin buzzing around your system without adding even more stimulus for the racing heart and sweaty palms. Chocolate and cola drinks, unfortunately, also come under this banner.

I have vivid memories of a physiology lesson at University in which we learnt about the varying effects that certain drinks have on our metabolism. We each had to drink a measured volume of liquid as quickly as we could, then over the next three-hour period, collect any urine that we passed, record its volume and measure its salt content.

In groups of four, we had been allocated a litre of either Coca-Cola, saline (salty water), an isotonic drink (like Lucozade) or my choice – a litre of beer. I remember sliding down the wall of the laboratory, giggling with the other 'beer drinkers' and for the first time ever, finding my physiology teacher attractive!

Believe me, alcohol does not help you with your performance! Research in the library a couple of days later taught me much about the properties of diuretics like tea, coffee and beer and how they take water away from your body.

You're probably curious about the results of the experiment. Well, content-wise, the beer drinker passed the greatest volume of urine, closely followed by the Coca-Cola drinker. The saline drinker had the greatest change in salt concentration, and a strangely good time was had by all!

Milk

Jason Vale, author of *The Juice Master's Ultimate Fast Food*, has a really interesting section in his book about milk. He says:

'Milk contains a protein called Casein, which is chemically bound to calcium. To digest milk properly we need enzymes that we haven't had in our systems since we were three years old. Casein is used as the base for one of the strongest wood glues! Alarmingly, cow's milk has over 300 times more casein than human milk. It sticks to the walls of the stomach and prevents the good stuff you consume from being properly absorbed. Furthermore it hinders the elimination of waste.

Goat's milk, however, is produced by an animal that, like us, has only one stomach and can therefore be more easily digested by our bodies.'

Jason informs us that the Chinese consume no cow's milk at all and have among the lowest rates of osteoporosis, also that it is the humble onion that is the best bet against weak bones, not milk!

Laugh It Off

You will have gathered by now that I read a lot of books.

When I first read *Feel the Fear and Do It Anyway* by Susan Jeffers, I remember her comment that our body cannot tell the difference between a laugh that is formed naturally and one which is forced. She advocated laughing out loud to produce 'feel-good' hormones in the body.

Not long after my car crash when I was finding life rather tough, I remember driving to work and forcing myself to try this. I remember thinking that I had nothing to lose. I felt a little daft as I began and hoped that I would not have to stop at the approaching traffic lights. After a while the smile on my face was natural rather than forced, so it worked.

Since that time I have heard and read much more about the health benefits of laughter therapy. Robert Holden has devoted his career to this subject with *The Happiness Project*. His website www.happiness.co.uk has a wealth of resources.

Laughing boosts your happy hormones – the endorphins. As the level increases it makes you feel good. Several hospitals in America take the effects of laughter so seriously they have designed 'laughter rooms' where a doctor leads the way in laughing out loud. The patients follow suit and they have found their recovery rate is increased by following this therapy. Knowing that this is the effect, the next time that you are about to face a scenario that scares you, perhaps you could listen to something en route that would make you laugh.

Allow yourself a break with laughter! Take out your Billy Connolly video or whatever causes you to laugh out loud, and give yourself a boost. Laughter really can be the best medicine.

Sleep, Rest and Relaxation
Sleep helps to refresh the body and the mind. According to Peter Walters, Assistant Professor in Kinesiology at Wheaton University in the US,

Mental functioning decreases twice as rapidly as physical performance with lack of sleep.

Disturbed sleep can make you irritable, makes it hard for you to concentrate, decreases your creativity and, of course, exhausts you. Maximum needs for sleep can vary a lot from person to person. Being aware of what your optimal needs are and honouring them, will help you in your quest to conquer fear.

Sleep Inducers

- Reduce caffeine intake before sleeping; instead have warm drinks that have a more sedative effect such as hot milk, herbal teas or caffeine-free hot drinks.

- Stick to a regular time for sleep as much as you can.

- Wind down half an hour to one hour before sleeping and avoid mentally stimulating pursuits before going to bed.

- Avoid eating meals close to bedtime, and if you want a late night snack, eat complex carbohydrates such as bread rather than foods filled with sugar.

- Take physical exercise during the day to tire your body, rid your system of toxins and promote sleep.

- Reduce muscular tension with a bath, massage or relaxation tape before bed.

- Reduce alcohol intake as it is filled with sugar and acts as a stimulant.

A mug of camomile tea works best for me and also remembering to stop work more than half an hour before I want to go to sleep.

Relaxation

We all have our own preferred methods of relaxation; although you may not have taken time to think about a specific strategy to unwind.

Playing a piano and using the computer are two of the main culprits for causing muscle tension in my shoulders and arms. The Jacuzzi at my local gym has always been a good antidote to this providing welcome relief, and a suitable reward after hours of work.

When pushing your boundaries, rest and relaxation is an important part of the process. Without the climb down from that which causes stress, the results can at worst be fatal. The pages of the newspapers provide us with many sad examples of what happens when someone ignores this and prematurely leaves this world as a result of a heart attack or stroke.

Essential Oils
I think it is safe to say that our sense of smell is the least utilised of our senses. Again, I'm no expert in this field, but I experienced first-hand the difference that oils can make through aromatherapy massage and by using them in an oil burner at home. As with the food section, I bring to you an abbreviated version of what I have learnt. For a more thorough insight into this subject, please take a look at the recommended text in the resource section at the end of the book.

Some essential oils have properties that can help to reduce tense, nervous feelings. Most people can easily get hold of essential oils these days and simply having a bottle of good lavender oil can serve a number of purposes. In its mildest form it is a relaxant, but used in larger quantities lavender can be a stimulant too. Lavender is also a natural antibiotic and, if used in an oil burner, can boost your immune system and kill off any bugs in the air that might have otherwise given you a cold.

I add a few drops of lavender to my bath when I want to relax. I also use it when I want to avoid infection. Working as an Optician requires that I get very close to patients. Often in the winter they will have colds. If I burn lavender in the room where

I work, the antibiotic properties help to ward off infection and help me to stay healthy. I also have used it in the past to help me to relax at a piano concert. By putting a few drops of the oil on a hanky, if I breathe in the scent it helps me to calm down and relax more than I could with thoughts alone.

In her book, *The Fragrant Pharmacy*, Valerie Ann Worwood writes that:

'Essential oils operate effectively not only on the cellular and physical level, but also in the emotional, intellectual and spiritual and aesthetic areas of our lives. Essential oils can be applied through the skin – in massage oils, or by osmosis in the bath, or by inhalation in a variety of methods.

The way to health is to have an aromatic bath and scented massage every day.

As far back as 4th Century BC Hippocrates recognised that burning certain aromatic substances offered protection against contagious diseases. In fact, the positive effects of essential oils on blood circulation are well known for they play an important role in bringing oxygen and nutrients to the tissues while assisting in the efficient disposal of carbon dioxide and the other waste cell products that are produced by cell metabolism. This general increase in blood flow improves the efficiency of the immune system.'

Which Oils Help?

There are many different oils with differing properties that can help you to feel a certain way. The best way to learn about them for me has been via direct contact with a qualified aromatherapist. A massage from someone in this field will include a mini education about which oils help with different problems.

What's the Piano in Your Life?

Having heard about a whole variety of ways in which you can minimise the effects of feeling fear, it is time for you to consider how you can put this knowledge to use, for it is only when you feel the symptoms that you will get to find out which of the techniques work for you.

Summary

- Make the best use of mental and physical preparation of your body.

- Practise the techniques that will allow you to control your state so that you can psych yourself up, or calm yourself down at will, to be able to produce your best performance.

- Honour your biological needs for food. Choose that which will give you stability as far as your sugar levels are concerned.

- Make sure you care for yourself well by getting the exercise, and rest that you need as well as working hard at practising your skills.

- Use what you know about the other factors like aromatherapy, laughter, and positive self-talk to also help you.

9 | Stepping Beyond the Comfort Zone

It is only when we make mistakes in performance that we can really begin to notice what needs attention.

Rosamund Stone Zander & Benjamin Zander, authors of
The Art of Possibility – Transforming the Professional and Personal Life.

Playing a piano in my living room was one thing, performing to a huge, fee paying audience at a concert was completely another. By engineering intervals between those two places I was able to make the transition less of a shock to the system.

Each new step that progressively expanded my comfort zone made me sweat and feel uncomfortable the first time I tried it, but repeated exposure to those feelings diminished their effect. Each of the intermediate steps taught me valuable lessons about my ability and myself. Each showed me what aspects of my character or the piece of music, still needed more practice.

It began with something as simple as using a recording device to listen back to my performance and progressed through steps that involved other people listening to me at home. Playing the piano in public places was the next step and eventually became more of a game than the trial I had felt I was enduring in the very early days.

Whatever skill you are learning to expand, there will be transition steps that you can take which will mirror this path of

185

growth in ability. As you progressively expose yourself by expanding your comfort zone, it will help to strengthen your belief in yourself. This in turn, will contribute to the speed of progress you make and your ability to take bigger, bolder steps forward.

In Chapter 7 I talked about practising your skill and having consideration for how and where you learn. The focus of this section is aimed more at stretching and strengthening those foundations to enable you to deal with the greater pressure and attention from an audience.

As you read about these intervals think about how you can apply the concept to your own challenge and the strategy you can devise.

- How and where to increase the pressure
- Mental and physical rehearsals
- The Performance

In Chapter 8 we looked at what happens to our performance once symptoms of fear arise. The graph on page 167 showed how the level of arousal that we feel can impact the severity of the fear symptoms. By increasing the pressure step-by-step the aim is to move the slope of the graph to the right. This means that a scenario, which at one time caused distress, with practice and by pushing your comfort boundaries, will now fall in an area that leaves you feeling dynamic.

The end result of these steps has to be feeling more comfortable with ever-increasing demands on your talent and ability. So the goal is expanding not only what you can do, but also how and where you can do it!

How to Increase the Pressure

I challenged my ability with the music by varying a number of things:

Speed

A metronome is a device that ticks like a very loud clock. This helps you to keep a constant speed as you play your piece of music. It can be set to almost any speed, whether slow and measured or quick and lively. The tendency to speed up when performing under pressure (a common occurrence once the fight or flight mechanisms have kicked in), is challenged and controlled by training alongside this.

Deliberately setting a faster speed than I am used to will force errors in the parts of the music that need more attention. Slowing it down can give me time as I play to think about including more variety and emotion into the performance.

Charles Rosen, author of *Piano Notes*, suggests that it is important to drive your learning into your subconscious. He suggests learning to play a piece of music whilst at the same time occupying or distracting your conscious mind. For example, by reading a simple book at the same time as practising a musical phrase over and over. I tried this and found it extremely difficult, but I can appreciate the potential value here and offer it as a tool that may help some of you.

Another method taught by one of my piano teachers was to count out loud whilst playing the piece. Having to concentrate on what number comes next as well as reading the music is a way of overloading your conscious mind so that the subconscious also has to take part. Both of these methods drive the learning deeper and, therefore, should allow the performance to hold up under the pressure of public performance. This way your subconscious can carry you through even if your conscious mind becomes distracted.

If you are learning to sing a song or give a presentation, there are similar things that you could do to vary the pace of delivery to also find weak spots, and to play about with the content, or props that you might use.

Yourself

are in the comfort of your own home, this will
of tension to your performance. All of a sudden the
ndard and the smoothness of delivery reduce as you are
aware that you are going to listen to it once you have finished.
I have learnt a tremendous amount from using this technique
and I know I always feel uncomfortable as I start to listen
back to the performance. But, I could never hope to learn as
much from just paying attention as I go along. After a couple
of occasions hearing the result and working with it, it does feel
more natural.

I have a 'record' button on my digital piano that I use when I
want to listen to what I have practised. There are many ways
that you can record sound these days;

You can download a free software programme for your computer called Audacity. It has the facility to record and edit. All
you need is a microphone that you can plug into your computer. It is available from www.audacity.com

There are also many fairly inexpensive portable recording
devices available. The digital versions easily plug into your
computer for you to download what you have recorded to
keep for future use, or transfer to a CD, should you wish.

If you don't have a computer there's still no excuse. Be creative!
Use your mobile phone, or your landline answer machine to
record the performance, and then call yourself to listen back.

Your objective is to listen to your performance in order to
find out what works well, and where more practice is needed.
What you hear will be quite different to what you imagine it
should sound like.

When you listen back to the recording you hear your performance as your potential audience is likely to hear it. Whilst you

are playing or speaking your focus is on what comes next and how you are interpreting it. The points where you are unsure of the material will become obvious and you will hear any hesitation once you listen back.

The first time you listen to the performance, just take it in as a whole and get an overall impression. Try to listen in an un-biased and non-judgemental way. Listen a second time armed with a pencil in your hand, ready to mark on the music score or your script, where you hesitate or stumble, or any points that seem to drag on for too long. Write down specifically what you want to do differently to improve it. There might be just one or two places that really need work to make the difference between an 'ok' performance and a 'great' one.

I have found this tool one of the most valuable for improving speaking presentations. I learn more from watching a video or hearing a recording of myself than I ever could learn from someone telling me what they liked and disliked. As I revise each version of my speech or piano piece I then record the new version to see if the result I have achieved is as I intended.

Video
This provides yet another learning opportunity. I was amazed at what I saw on a video after I recorded a piano perform-ance at a concert. I hadn't thought previously about using this technique to judge 'what not to wear' but I made an instant decision from watching a particular performance that I will NEVER wear a skirt that comes above my knees again, whilst I play a piano on stage! I didn't quite bare all, but it was far too much for my liking!

Until I watched a video, I wasn't aware that I sat bolt upright and very still when playing in front of an audience. One of my pet dislikes is to watch musicians who move what I consider 'too much,' and really over dramatise the whole thing. However, watching video footage of myself performing, I was very much at the opposite end of the scale and my body language gave the impression of tension and fear. This is not what I w. nted to convey whether it was true or not! Seeing myself stiff like this gave me an opportunity to work on actually moving as I perform. In practice sessions at home I would over emphasise the movements and have fun with it. Once on stage again, although the movement was a lot less, at least there was some and the result was that I looked, sounded and felt more confident. On the speaking platform too, this can make a massive difference.

After a bit of self-analysis, make a point of learning from what other performers do. Take yourself off to a concert or conference and watch. Enjoy the presentations, but also see how the artist or speaker performs and what it is that engages you in their performance – not only words or music, but their gestures, the variety of facial expressions, the whole set up of the event, how they walk on stage. Notice all the aspects of the performance. Do not feel guilty for being there rather than practising yourself. This is all part of the essential learning experience if you are to truly give performance your best shot.

How might you record what you need to do?

How might you speed up or slow down the performance to help you find weak areas or add more flavour to what you do?

Create an Audience

If part of your challenge involves an audience watching your performance, then at some point you need to 'expose yourself' and there has to be practice with an audience present. It's unwise to wait until the real thing to have your first run through with other people listening.

If you let your imagination loose then there are lots of places that you can manufacture an audience.

Suggestions for Where You Might Find an Audience

Ask the next person who calls you on the phone if they would be willing to listen, even if they are a complete stranger! A good experience has always come of this method for me. It feels daft at first, but part of the point of this is getting used to feeling uncomfortable and being able to perform regardless. Put the phone on loudspeaker and play or stand up and deliver your presentation. (And do remember to hit the 'record' button on your dictation machine at the same time – if you have one!)

Invite the neighbours round to listen to you. A friendly audience is always a good place to start.

Find a group of willing people to perform to. Where? There are audiences all around you if you are willing to look.

If like me you play a piano, you might find one in a local music shop, or in a hotel. If your instrument is portable, what would it take for you to perform in the high street? If this is too far outside your comfort zone, think about what steps you could put in between such that you might eventually consider it. If you don't want to be recognised or remembered, drive to somewhere a bit further afield. Take a friend with you for moral support – one who you know will hold you to your word about what you want to do and provide you with the comfort of a friendly face.

If you are perfecting a speech, what opportunities could you find to perform to a small group of people? Is there a club that meets locally that might appreciate your performance or presentation? Could you speak at a Chamber of Commerce event or at a networking meeting? With a bit of lateral thinking you will find plenty of audiences to practise on!

Get Some Feedback

Beyond finding an audience to listen to you, comments from a well-seasoned expert in your field could also help you take your performance up a notch or two. If you are a musician, find someone who really knows what performance is all about. Choose someone who you know and trust or someone recommended to you. What you are after is positive constructive feedback to give you another perspective about how you might improve your performance.

Be careful from where you seek advice. Ask it of those whom you admire and respect. There is no point getting feedback from a person whose style is not one that you would want to emulate.

With writing this book, allowing other people to see my work was a challenge at first. I would be reluctant to let it go and get feedback. Whatever the skill you intend to work on, exposing yourself (in the nicest possible way) to outside opinion is essential, if you want your ability to grow.

Expand what you are comfortable with so that you increase the pressure slowly. The aim is to create good experiences, not to push so hard that you make a mess and have a bigger psychological barrier to overcome than before.

Recording your performance once you have an audience will highlight different areas of strengths and weaknesses to those you will have discovered recording without one, so ensure that you have a recording device present for this part too.

Anticipate Distractions

During a concert or a public performance there are many things that could potentially happen to distract your attention and throw your performance off balance. By thinking about a few of these and working them into your practice routine, it will be yet another way to bolster and secure your end performance.

In front of one of your manufactured, friendly audiences, ask them to create a few distractions like coughing, getting up and moving, taking a phone call. Explain why you are doing this and what you hope to achieve as a result.

As a speaker I had experience at dealing with distractions. When I was a member of Toastmasters in Perth, Western Australia, there was a club that I went to which held dinner meetings. The waiter would bring out the meals as the presentations continued, so people would be eating their food during the speech. I found this really annoying initially, but when someone explained the value of the distraction to me, in that you had to listen harder to stay focused on the story, and as a speaker, you had to be able to continue beyond the distraction – I was able to reframe the irritation to a welcomed challenge to be conquered.

I was not quite so well prepared from the piano perspective – hence the inclusion of this section! Learn from my omission. During the performance that I gave at the Professional Speakers convention, the audience started clapping along to the piano music, out of time and faster than I wanted to play! More about what happened follows in the next chapter.

I was proud of the lengths I had gone to in order to be ready, but hindsight will always allow you to discover yet one more thing that could've made a positive difference. Each of the things that we learn though can add strength to the strategy that we follow before the next event. So make a plan for what might happen and include some practice sessions to deal with it.

Visualise yourself in the room where you will perform or speak as you hit the 'record' button and it will add just a little more pressure. Rehearsing in your mind how you will walk onto the stage and mentally rehearsing your final performance can start from a very early stage. Your body will learn to associate with those images and allow you to feel more familiar when you reach your final destination. The chemical reaction in our bodies can be influenced by thoughts as much as reality. This is how people worry themselves sick, but equally we could use this phenomenon to boost ourselves up and give ourselves good feelings with respect to the approaching event.

Where to Increase the Pressure

Get Used to Unfamiliar Surroundings

Changing the environment in which you perform will add a sense of unease that you can't replicate in the comfort of your own home. I made a vow to myself very early on in this quest to play a piano whenever and wherever I saw one. That commitment stands to this day. Once you start looking for places to perform, you will be amazed at the vast number of ideas and also how weird and wacky your imagination can be!

Playing the £25,000 pianos dating from 1890, in the basement at Liberty's has to be one of the most privileged of those occasions. Nearly being thrown out of a hotel in Dubai for daring to touch the piano was one of the less favourable memories!

By becoming familiar with playing in many unfamiliar places, I learnt how to feel more comfortable with feeling uncomfortable when someone else was within earshot. This had a massive positive impact when the concert performances finally came around.

What other aspects of your performance can be rehearsed?

Practise the Entrance and Exit
The entrance from stage left or right, taking a bow, the clothes and shoes that are to be worn for the performance, are all aspects that can be rehearsed.

I had a full dress rehearsal practising all the above at the house of a local farmer – Norman Beeby. It felt odd to go round there in all my glad rags and my high heels, to make an entrance into his living room, bow, sit and play, take the applause and leave. But when it came to the event, the feelings of discomfort and fear were more familiar to me having pushed my comfort zone to include this as part of my practice. I felt calmer and more confident knowing that I had taken this into account and done something about it.

Where could you rehearse what you need to do?

We practise to improve on our worst possible performance.
Dominic Alldis, Head of Jazz, Royal College of Music.

The Performance Itself

Things to Consider

Clothes: Choose your outfit for your performance carefully. Pick something that fits well, looks good, and makes you feel great! Start at the very beginning and if sexy underwear puts a smile on your face, then take advantage and wear it!

The height of the shoes you wear will affect how you walk, and, if you are playing a piano and using a pedal, it will affect how that feels beneath your feet. Get used to performing in some of your practice sessions wearing the shoes you will perform in. Even if you're not playing a piano, anything that requires you to move about will need to be practised in the appropriate shoes.

Check yourself on video to make sure that your clothes look how you hope they will. Try with your jacket open and then closed, which do you prefer, do you have a choice? Remember if you are to wear a lapel microphone you will need to have somewhere to attach the 'box' and this can affect how your outer clothes, such as your jacket, fit and look.

Lighting – be aware of how the lighting at your venue will affect you being seen. Where are the shaded and the light spots on the stage? Have someone give you guidance from the floor about where to position yourself for the best effect.

Unfamiliar equipment – if you are not using your own instrument or equipment, things will feel a little unusual and time taken to acquaint yourself is essential.

Microphones and amplifiers – it is crucial if your instrument or voice is to be given amplification that you get used to how this sounds BEFORE you have an audience. Make time for a sound check and rehearsal in advance of them arriving.

If you have a microphone attached to your clothes, be aware of the gestures that you use and how the sound will be picked up by it. Movement of your hand across where the microphone is attached will create a rustling sound that will be heard. This can be a distraction to you and your audience. If there is a point where you turn your head to the left and you are wearing your microphone on your right lapel, the volume and quality of the sound may be adversely affected. It is only by wearing the microphone and trying these things out that you will discover its limitations.

Having your piano, instrument or voice linked into an amplification system means that the sound that you produce will be heard from the speakers in the auditorium, rather than directly from you. This can be a major distraction if you are not used to it. Again learnt and shared with hindsight!

The first time my piano was linked up in this way to loud speakers, was during an important performance with Mo Shapiro as I played to accompany her singing. Our performance was the after dinner entertainment at the Institute of Customers Service's annual conference. Earlier that day when we rehearsed the song, I heard her voice and my piano from the speakers at the front of the stage and was OK with that. However, I practised my solo piece with headphones on, not wanting to take up any more of the sound engineer's time, and consequently didn't get to hear what I sounded like when performing alone.

To give Mo time to change her outfits between acts, I played my piano solo. On stage alone in a glittering ballroom, before an audience of 250 people, for the first time, as I started to play, I heard my piano booming from the speakers at the back of the room. This was a massive shock to the system even though logic would have me expect it. The thoughts that raced through my head were along the lines of, 'Oh s**t, that's me playing – better not mess up now!' Not the kind of thing I would recommend you say to yourself! The affirmation practice obviously needed more work! That thought no doubt prompted the part where I then froze. I threw my hands in the air, rolled my eyeballs to the ceiling, laughed, shrugged my shoulders and carried on. The audience laughed with me thinking it was all part of the act. Having made 'mistakes' on stage before, it came within my ability to be able to deal with it, and for that incident not to impact the rest of my perform-ance. People were left wondering if 'the mistake' was part of the act. I was flattered by the fact that they weren't sure.

I share this with you in the hope that it will prompt you to be more prepared for your event. These days, I ALWAYS make time for a full rehearsal with amplification if that is what is needed.

It is only with practice that you will bring a new skill confidently within your armoury.

Arrive Early
Allow plenty of time for traffic diversions, accidents, and delays. It is much better to have too much time than too little if you want to have a hope of putting pre-performance anxiety (reframed to excitement!) to use.

Also the earlier you arrive, the more time you have to make a connection with the sound crew, and the event organisers, to have a rehearsal and sound check.

Mind Management En Route
I talked about methods to psych yourself up or calm yourself down in Chapter 7. Remember to use them as you travel to the event. Make sure you have the appropriate CDs in your car to help you access the state that will enable you to produce your best performance.

Sometimes before an event, I have called a friend with NLP skills to help me to access and anchor feelings from previous events where I have felt and enjoyed success. Talking about what I felt, saw and heard makes the memory and feelings more vivid and brings them to the foreground for use at this current event. This process allows me to feel great confidence and has been a tremendous help. Of course practice makes perfect – the more times that you practise accessing this state, the less time it takes to access it when needed before a performance.

Try this for yourself by setting the scenario up with a friend. Get them to ask you questions about something that you know brings back great memories. This is how the conversation might have gone between us:

'Tracy, tell me about the best time you had when you went horse riding.' I would then tell the story.

My friend might then ask for more details like, 'What did it feel like? Where were you? What did you see? Tell me what you could hear?' By elaborating on the topic and engaging my senses of sight, sound and feeling the effect on the body is greater. Once I capture those feelings I can then turn the energy felt towards the event at which I am about to test my skills.

So my friend might then continue with 'How do you feel now? Where in your body do you feel that?' Once I have answered these questions, he might continue, 'Remember how great that feeling is. Know that you can call on that at any time just by thinking about that great time.'

It is only by creating opportunities that stretch your comfort zone for performance that you will be able to practise the techniques and find out which methods of preparation will work best for you.

Playing in junior league football, no matter how much you train, will only prepare you for junior league. If you want to step up to the professional and public arena then that is where you will get your real experience of the game. Concert performances and paid speaking engagements are in a league beyond the confines of your home and the experience needed to be good at them comes only with repeated exposure on that 'playing field'.

What's the playing field on which you really need to rehearse?

Stepping on Stage

Before I am about to step on stage I will breathe deeply, making sure I exhale as far as I can. I will remember a previous time of success and think about the music or message that I want to share. I will remind myself about how well prepared I am and trust myself to do what I know I can do. It is time to enjoy the ride, share my passion, and receive the applause!

Head held high, shoulders down, standing tall, breathing deep, and beaming from ear to ear; I step out onto the stage...

What's the Piano in Your Life?

This is all very well in theory, but the time when you will really learn is when you put all these steps to use and translate them into action, and actually step outside your comfort zone to perform in front of an audience. Planning how you will expand your ability bit by bit will decrease the likelihood of taking a nosedive from which you have to recover before moving on. So, bearing in mind the steps outlined above, think about how you could use this approach. Stretching your comfort zone, by its very nature will feel uncomfortable – there is no way of avoiding this.

What steps could you take to increase pressure that will stretch your comfort zone and skill?

What is your first step and the next, and the next? Work it out, have a strategy.

Who could you talk to about it? Talking to others will bring about suggestions that you would never have thought of, that could make a great difference.

Summary

- Test the foundation – vary the speed and the location of your performance.

- Record yourself – on the phone, using a video, or a voice recorder.

- Create an audience – friends, neighbours, and strangers.

- Get expert feedback – from someone who knows more about your subject than you.

- Anticipate distractions – prepare for the unexpected and get used to things that might put you off.

- Change the environment – perform in unfamiliar places – get used to feeling uncomfortable in unfamiliar surroundings.

- Practise the entire performance – wear the clothes that you will perform in. Make your entrance, play/speak/sing whatever you need to do, receive applause, bow if appropriate and leave.

- Practice a highly successful virtual version in your mind over and over.

- Create opportunities that will expand your comfort zone and test your ability.

- Know what strategies will best serve you en route to the event.

- Allow plenty of time to get there.

- Have a rehearsal once at the venue, checking any equipment that you may need to use.

- Record your performance so that you can learn how to take it to the next level for the following event.

10 The Concerts

The only way of discovering the limits of the possible is to venture a little way past them into the impossible.

Arthur C. Clarke

Although I had tentatively 'exposed' myself by playing a piano in lots of different places, the concerts felt like a whole different ball game. It was time to put all the learning together, trust that I had done all that I could to prepare, and believe that I would pull it off and be successful.

There were many vulnerable moments. At times it felt like being in the eye of a storm. However, I emerged to find a glorious rainbow and sunshine on the other side in the form of far greater courage, self-belief, confidence and, of course, the ability to share my passion for piano music with other people.

Within one year of starting to take action I had played a solo piano performance in seven concerts. I was amazed at my speed of progress. Never before had I realised I had such a level of commitment and determination, but then I had never set myself a challenge quite like this.

The lessons that I learnt through the whole process have given me an incredibly elevated sense of my true ability when I follow a passion beyond the confines of my fear. Being able to share my passion for playing a piano with other people felt like jumping out of a box to freedom.

Despite all the preparation, I was not immune to the feelings of fear and had to face them on many occasions. I learned how to maintain a good standard of performance in spite of them. I also learnt how to enjoy the thrill of the performance, although for the first few events I would not have worded it quite like that in the hours before I was due to perform.

The rewards were many. They came in the form of far greater wisdom and understanding of myself and of course the joy of accomplishing my goal – to conquer my fear of playing the piano in public. The universal lessons I took away, extend way beyond the keys of a piano.

As you read about what ultimately happened I invite you to keep a couple of questions at the back of your mind:

- Where is fear stopping me doing something I would really love to do?

- What do I stand to gain if I tackle it head on and take some action?

Concerns and Feeling the Fear
As I approached the concerts the main opponent was the inner battle with my mind. The physical symptoms of fear still felt very real and served to remind me that I could not kid myself as to how I felt about the approaching events.

The night before a performance I would lie in bed trying to sleep, with my hand resting on my stomach hoping that its warmth would stop the churning. I would wake with a start the morning of the event with the realisation that this was THE day of the performance. Throughout the day, I would be too nervous to touch the piano keys at home. I always waited until I was at the venue to rehearse and warm up my fingers.

In Chapter 8 I talked about the NLP technique of re-framing which re-labels nervous feelings to those of 'excitement.' I can't claim that I was able to keep this interpretation firmly in my mind before the first few concerts. I was aware of it and would remind myself of the technique as I headed along the corridor to the ladies loo 'just one more time.' It was only with time and increasing the frequency of performances, that I was able to make effective use of this technique. So take heart that you are not alone if you still feel nervous before a performance or a big event of some kind. Even some of the most seasoned performers continue to feel this way. They say that once you no longer feel that anticipation, then you may as well quit because it's obviously no longer important to you!

A few times before playing in the earlier few concerts, I felt like I was on autopilot. It was almost like an out-of-body experience where you can see yourself but don't fully feel a part of what's going on. Arriving at the event, I would feel completely numb. This unnerved me in the beginning, but as I came to recognise this as a normal reaction for me, I was less concerned by it.

Apply yourself. Get all the education you can, but then, by God, do something. Don't just stand there, make it happen.

Lee Iacocca

Scary Moments

The first concert performance was an 'Old Time Music Hall' event at the smallest theatre I have ever seen, in a hard-to-find suburb of Sheffield. It was a little tired in its appearance and had obviously been well used over the years. It had the traditional seats covered in red velvet, and peeling gold leaf adorned crumbling but ornate plasterwork on the walls and ceilings. The theatre was full to capacity with about 60 people who all looked like they would appreciate a bit more space between the seats.

My family were in the audience and my worst fear was that if I made a mistake and ended up humiliating myself, there would forever be someone in my life who would be a reminder of that fate to me. I remember thinking that it would be safer if no one knew me or was ever going to see me again. I was to be fourth on in the first half playing Scott Joplin's *Maple Leaf Rag*.

When I initially wrote this chapter I had described it as being 'fun!' I re-read my words months later and laughed out loud when I saw what I had written. Looking back can often offer quite a distorted view. Our memories can sometimes forget the pain, thank goodness, or we might never move on. A more realistic description was that it was scary! It definitely had my stomach churning and my palms sweating. I went to my diaries to bring you a more realistic take on it.

> *Tomorrow is a big day. I can hardly believe that I am going to go on stage and voluntarily play a piano in front of a crowd of people. I have been talking about it for a while and it feels like a story that I tell, but not that it's really real.*

> *I remember feeling that way when I was telling people that I was moving to Australia. I know I can do it, I feel excited, nervous, proud, scared. I am going to go up there and just give it all I've got.*

(Written the day after the concert)

> *I arrived early for the dress rehearsal and felt oddly detached, but confident.*

> *Later that evening as I sat in the audience waiting for my turn I wasn't preoccupied with the performance, I felt slightly apprehensive, a bit excited, but calm in the knowledge that I'd done all I could and I'd give it my best shot.*

As my friend Stuart introduced me I took a deep breath and walked confidently on stage, smile fixed firmly in place. As I began to play, I was proud that I was doing well – all the difficult bits that I'd spent hours practising came out nimbly beneath my fingers. But all of a sudden, just like when I was ten years old, I froze.

It was like someone had pulled the plug out of the socket again and the cord that linked my hands to my brain was gone. I don't know what possessed me but I lifted my hands from the keys, and with my left hand waved at the audience and then carried on playing.

I am told that I had a big smile on my face for the rest of the performance and that the applause was louder for me than for anyone else. When I got down off the stage, I couldn't remember taking the applause or actually walking back to my seat – it was like being on automatic pilot then suddenly being transported back into my own body. I remember breathing out as I sat down in my chair and wondering whether I had forgotten to breathe the whole time I was playing.

People came up to me afterwards to say that they had really enjoyed my piece, that it sounded very intricate and clever. One of them asked, 'That mistake in the middle – was it deliberate?' I laughed and smiled at his question wondering how someone could think that.

'Thank you,' I answered, 'but no, it wasn't deliberate, but I'm so glad you thought it might have been.''

I did not remember my mistake every time I saw my parents. After the concert I was expecting them to be really proud of me for finally being able to play a piano in public. Although they both said it was a nice concert, they made no mention of what I had accomplished. I don't think to this day they really understand what a huge leap it was for me to play in front of that audience or the many others that I undertook. For me though, this was a MASSIVE triumph and I felt very proud.

What I Learnt

- Even if I make a mistake and/or freeze, I have the confidence and ability to carry on.

- My whole performance will not be judged by a mistake.

- Not everyone will recognise the importance and significance to me, of my goals, nor their achievement.

- I needed to become more aware of my breathing under concert conditions so that I could think clearly and actually take it all in.

Blowing Hot and Cold

The second concert followed just two weeks later at a much larger and very grand theatre in Shepherd's Bush, London. There were over a hundred people in the audience. The event was to be a combination of professionals and amateurs like myself. Most of the people who were to perform I knew from a self-development course in team leadership and management that I was a part of (as I mentioned in Chapter 4.)

My biggest concern about this one was the contrast in ability between the professionals and myself. In particular the difference between how my own performance would compare to that of my teacher Maria, (who you will remember was trained at the Moscow School of Music.) Her performance was due to follow mine and close the first half. I was also concerned about the fact that people were paying money to hear us play. They had paid when I performed in the first concert, but it hadn't really occurred to me at that time.

I had arranged for the whole event to be recorded on video because I wanted physical proof, that I could watch again and again, which proved that I could play in public. It hadn't occurred to me to ask someone to record that first event and I am sad to have missed an opportunity to have on film such a breakthrough and landmark achievement in my life, (which is why I am so fervent at encouraging you to capture what you can as you go along.)

Once at the venue, there were a couple of hours of rehearsals and sound checks for everyone before we were all sent to change into our outfits for the concert. The sense of excitement and anticipation was immense. Once I was ready in my poshest performance dinner suit and wearing the sparkly sequinned top that I had bought back from Melbourne, I called my friend Michael Tipper for a bit of moral support. He used one of the NLP exercises that I mentioned in Chapter 9, to help me get into a really strong and resourceful frame of mind.

As I walked back into the foyer dressed and mentally ready for the challenge ahead, I was greeted by my friend Pam, who I hadn't seen for about a year. Pam wanted to buy me a drink and I found temptation and my thirst so great that I couldn't resist joining her by accepting a gin and tonic. When I sat down on the front row next to my teacher, Maria, I received an icy glare as she reminded me that the drink would interfere with my performance and would make my hands sweat. So I settled for just one sip as I sat down next to her, knowing that she was right.

While I was waiting for my turn I felt alternately really hot or really cold. When I was hot, I took my jacket off. My arms would then be exposed and I would get cold, so I put the jacket back on. And so it continued over and over.

The chairs that we were sat on had cold metallic steel frames painted gold with plush red velvet cushions on top. When my hands were hot I would press them against the cold metal to cool them down, and when they got too cold, I would tuck them under my arms to try to warm them up. My right hand is still difficult to warm up as a result of the injuries from the crash. It felt like someone was playing with my body temperature on the end of a yo-yo.

When it was my turn to play, the hall suddenly seemed to echo with silence and the piano seemed bigger all of a sudden. Walking over to it, I sat down, took a deep breath, paused as I held my hands over the keys and then started to play. After no more than a few seconds, I faltered, blushed, stopped, apologised, and said, 'I'll start again'. That time I got through it. When I finished, the applause really warmed my heart. I was so relieved, and this time, I was able to take in the smiling faces and enjoy the appreciation for a moment before returning to my seat.

Maria smiled and mouthed 'Well done' as she got up to take her turn at the keys. The music that she played was haunting and full of emotion. It had us all sitting wide-eyed, silent, and mesmerized by her skill and dexterity. Her ability as a concert pianist could never be in dispute and has to be seen and heard to be fully appreciated.

My gin and tonic was the best ever accompaniment to that performance that you can imagine. When she finally finished, there was silence for a few seconds as everyone came out of the trance the music had put them in, then rapturous applause filled the air.

I felt very proud to have been the reason for her being there so she could share with everyone the pleasure of her music … and all because of a chance meeting in a piano shop.

What I Learnt

- Don't drink alcohol before a performance, but really enjoy a drink as a reward after the event! If you don't drink have another treat ready for after your achievement.

- That when I falter, I will survive!

- Video evidence provides undisputable evidence to boost your belief.

Once you start taking steps outside your comfort zone, don't be tempted to pause for a rest. Take advantage of the rush of adrenalin that feels like energy from the crest of a wave and keep going!

Feeling More Relaxed

Opportunity number three occurred at a wedding of two friends, Chris and Naomi. They wanted to have a show as part of their wedding reception where everyone who was a guest, and who possessed a talent, would have an opportunity to perform. The acts ranged from a youngster tap dancing, to Chris's 88-year-old grandma playing a piano duet with his Mum. Chris played a guitar and sang with his brother, two women sang a duet accompanied by someone on the piano, and I played my Scott Joplin Ragtime piece again.

I was a lot more relaxed for this event and it was nice to experience how different it could feel to approach a piano without the level of fear that I had known from the previous two events. My performance was also a lot more relaxed and free of mistakes or hesitation this time. I actually enjoyed it rather than enduring it. As I took the applause and walked back to my chair, I was determined to find a way to take that relaxed nature with me to the other more formal events.

It was all recorded on CD and it was a wonderful surprise to be sent a copy with a 'thank you' note after the event.

What I Learnt

- There is a huge difference in how I enjoy the performance if I feel comfortable and relaxed.

- I am a lot less likely to make a mistake by being relaxed.

- CD proof of the sound of my performance when relaxed helped me to focus on how to achieve the same result elsewhere.

As you organise events to stretch your ability there is much to be learnt by having a variety of settings. If every event has a huge stress level attached to it, you will not necessarily learn in the fastest way.

Tears and Shaking Hands

The fourth concert was an end-of-term event at Loughborough College of Music where I had some of my piano lessons. All the pupils were to perform as part of their accreditation.

At the actual concert, my nerves did not overwhelm me, however, the morning of the event, I do remember crying in the shower at the prospect of what I was about to do and wondering why I was putting myself through all this stress.

I remember asking myself what I thought I was really going to achieve, apart from more grey hairs and weight loss, from forcing myself to play a piano in public. It felt like there were two different opinions within me. My brain told me that I had done lots of practice and would be fine, but within me there were still glimpses of the scared child who hated to play in front of anyone.

With the number of times I had played for people by then you might question as I did, how come I felt that way? This just demonstrates that we all have doubts, which can at times feel overwhelming, but we can overcome them. My performance was much better than my doubting self expected!

I was working that day as an Optician and so the nerves from the shower were soon forgotten as I drove to work and got on with my day-job. The drive to the venue after work was a bit rushed. I had to go home and change first. I had guests coming along as I had invited my family and my neighbours, Nellie and Arthur who had been my first invited 'audience' when I was still pushing my comfort zone in the comfort of my own home.

As I arrived at the college, rehearsals were well under way but running very late. The college band was still rehearsing as the audience began to file in. I didn't get to even touch the piano I was to perform on until half the audience had taken their seats.

Every piano feels really different to play. Although the notes are in the same place, the keys can be harder to press down and the pedals can have varying effects. It's not just a case of striking the right notes at the right time, but also knowing how hard they need to be pressed to achieve the sound required. I was fortunate that my practice noise was covered by the chap playing the drums very loudly just behind me.

My guests were late and frantic calls via mobile phone let me know that there was a line missing from my directions to the college. When they finally arrived only minutes before the concert started, it took a while for me to be able to shift my thoughts from guilt at having caused them inconvenience, to paying attention to what I needed for the performance.

I sat in the audience with them until it was my turn to play. As I approached the stage and the piano to a hushed auditorium, I sat on the stool and tried to adjust its height. But the last person to play had wound it so tight it would not budge. Feeling a bit uncomfortable because I wasn't as high up in relation to the keys as I wanted to be, I started playing with a steady pace so as not to trip up. That worked in the beginning; however, half way through, I was horrified when my hands started shaking uncontrollably.

It was almost as if I was watching them and they weren't connected to my body. It felt like they were playing without my instruction. I had experienced my knees knocking, as you heard about in my Dutch story in Chapter 4, and I was shaking when I played for Alvin and his daughter in Melbourne, but never before had my hands quivered quite like this. I was amazed that I was able to continue to play without it hampering the performance. As I left the stage and again was able to take in the applause, I wandered back to my seat hardly able to believe what had happened.

What I Learnt

- The outburst of emotion in the shower surprised my rational mind, but I learnt that even if I succumb to feeling so nervous that I cry, with something to occupy and distract my mind, I can change how I feel and still perform.

- There are things that can be done to minimise how nervous I feel. The fewer things that contribute to my stress levels, the calmer I will be. In this situation these would have been; giving more explicit instructions to my guests; being able to practise before the audience sat down; and making sure I can get the piano stool to the height I need it.

- If things don't go according to plan, it may increase the symptoms of nerves, but I have enough experience to come through in spite of that.

- That even if my hands start to shake, the learning is deep enough in my subconscious to make it possible to still complete the performance.

Sometimes you need for things to 'go wrong' for you to be able to learn the greatest lessons. This is when you truly get to find out how well the preparation has been done and it will help you discover what you need to do to be even better prepared in the future.

Without this kind of learning you are not really testing the boundaries of your comfort zone and learning how to stretch beyond it. However, there has to be caution when striding a long way out of your comfort zone as too hard a fall could potentially set you further back mentally. Also there is a risk that your relationship with yourself may suffer if you push too hard.

A friend commented to me that in pushing myself to the point where I was crying with fear of performance, I was repeating the act of my father in forcing me to play when I hadn't wanted to as a child. Sometimes we have to be cruel to be kind, but there also has to be a point where we learn to honour and respect our own needs.

Scoring 9/10 From a Business Audience

The ripple effects of stretching my comfort zone with regard to playing a piano had an impact on other areas of my life too. My keynote presentation that recounts the story and strategies from this book was developed to its current form during that year of transition. The piano played a key part (pun intended!) The first time it was delivered in a professional capacity was to a group in Leeds who are part of an organisation called The Academy of Chief Executives.

The presentation went really well, I was relaxed and the members of the group were very forthcoming when I invited them to talk about what my story evoked for them. They were very proactive with ideas based around my strategies as we created a plan of action to help one of the group quit smoking.

When it came to the piano piece, I played as I had before and there were only a couple of notes that went awry, but I had not stopped or had to start again.

I had fantastic feedback from the group. At the end of the session the speaker is graded out of 10 as each person in the group gives feedback to say what they thought of it. Every one of them gave me 9. In his concluding remarks the organiser, Jeff Monks, told me that this was very rare. They said the reason for the high score was that they got something that they could use in their own life from my story.

One of the group sought me out at the end to say that he thought it was such a shame that I beat myself up so much for making a mistake when I played the Scott Joplin piece. He said that my face gave away the pain that I felt and that, for him, it made me more human because it wasn't note perfect, but that it did not detract from the message one iota.

Since that day, I have made a point of smiling throughout the piano piece, regardless of what happens – not one of those false smiles that you might see on a stage, but a smile that demonstrates how proud I am and how glad I am that I can still play a piano.

What I Learnt

- A note played in error does not detract from the overall presentation.
- I have a powerful message in my story that can have a positive impact on the lives of other people.
- Putting into practice skills to boost my ability to conquer fear and increase my confidence playing a piano has a huge knock-on effect across all other areas of my life.

Sometimes the biggest learning will come from insights that other people provide you with. Make sure that you catch them with open arms and a grateful smile. Also in aspiring to push the boundaries of our own comfort zone we provide inspiration for others around us. Do not be afraid to share your stories of your achievements. They can be just the spark of inspiration that allows another person to take their next great leap forward.

The Retirement Home

During the time of this challenge, my Mum was working at a local retirement home. There was a piano there that one of the residents had brought with them when they moved in. Since this gentleman had passed away, it hadn't been played and people had commented about how they missed it. Mum told the story of what I was up to, and of course it was suggested that I play for the residents one afternoon. This event also became a presentation as I told them the story of my initial fear of performance, and the car crash that propelled me into action.

Before playing each piece of music I would tell them the story of why the piece meant something to me and of the memories that it held. My audience were eager to add their own comments and stories along the way too. It was a really enjoyable afternoon. Playing for such a grateful and contributing audience made my heart swell with pride. My Mum told me that they talked about it for many weeks. I felt very humble to have been able to make a difference if only for an hour or two.

What I Learnt

- When I do something in the service of others the reward far outweighs any discomfort I might feel.

- It was good to have another event to remind me about the benefits of playing in a relaxed state of mind, to prove that it wasn't a one-off occurrence.

- Making other people happy makes me feel good – more ammunition for my positive programming in the future.

- When I tell stories as well as play the piano, I feel a lot more relaxed about the performance.

Using your skills for the good of the community will do more than you think for the wellbeing of your soul. In this life where we are usually so short of time, making some available for the good of others, I promise, will bear a reward of greater value than its cost.

Dealing with Gremlins

The event, which all the former practice and concerts had been in aid of, was to open the Professional Speakers Convention as I mentioned back in the opening chapter. I was to play the piano to introduce the first keynote speaker – Steve McDermott. His presentation was to be about beliefs and how you can change them. I was his live example!

As I sat in the front row waiting for my cue to go on stage, I had the music score that I was to play, in my hands and was pouring over the first few notes repeating to myself, 'right hand D, left hand G, right hand D, left hand G'.

I was so scared that I would look at the piano and just go blank. I had intended to play without music, but the self-doubt and a flashback to the first time I tried to play the piece of music for Maria when I forgot where to start, saw me placing the music on the stand as I sat down to play. So much for all the positive mental conditioning I thought I had put into practice!

The introduction that I played went without a glitch and I sat back down after a minute and a half as Steve stepped onto the stage right on cue. The audience didn't know my story at that point.

Steve's presentation covered many stories about beliefs and how they can be changed. We heard stories about his children and notable people who had successfully challenged and changed a limiting belief. Then he came to me.

In a snapshot, he told them about my passion for playing a piano and of the fear that had held me back from performing as a youngster. He elaborated with the story of the crash, the broken hand and all the things that I had done since in order to vanquish the fear of playing for other people to such an extent that I could play before an international audience of speakers. He finished my story by saying,

'Some people attack their beliefs with this ...' and from behind the lectern he produced a small hacksaw,

'But some people', he said, again reaching behind the lectern, 'attack their beliefs with this ...' as he brought out a fully powered rotating chain saw which he revved a couple of times before saying,

'So please welcome back on stage to play some more ... Tracy Plaice!'

The fear was so much worse now that they knew the full story. My first introduction had been played in 'fake it' mode, now there was no hiding. Throughout Steve's speech I'd been frustrated for not trusting myself to find the first notes. When I returned to my piano, I threw the music I had left there down onto the floor in defiance of my former doubt. But as I began to play, very soon, there was a war going on in my head. The audience was so engrossed in the music that they started clapping along, out of time, and faster than I wanted to play! In my head I was screaming:

'NO!'

I began to make mistakes, but I kept going. It felt like I had an opponent on each shoulder. In one ear was a gremlin whispering, 'Quit now! They'll never know there was more.'

In the other ear was a little angel saying, 'You can do it; you know you can do it! You've played in seven concerts – keep going!'

I had gone to great lengths to be ready for this event, I had invited neighbours round, I had played in bars with football crowds listening, even a dress rehearsal at the local farmer's house, but I never thought to practise with someone clapping along. Hence the section in the last chapter about anticipating distractions! It put me right off!

Approaching the last line of the music my confidence grew. I knew I could play that blindfolded so I gave it all I had got; letting the final notes out with all the bravado I could muster. As I hit the last chord and looked up, the whole audience stood on their feet in rapturous applause. I came around from the

other side of the piano to take a bow and on walked Steve with the biggest bouquet of flowers that I have ever seen. The applause continued and I tingled from head to toe as I beamed at the audience. I felt very proud of myself as I sat back down in my seat. I could hardly believe I'd done it. A whole year of preparation to be ready and now it was done.

After Dinner Entertainment

There was more challenge to follow later that evening when I was also to play the piano to accompany my friend and colleague, Mo Shapiro, in her guise as Victoria Wood. We were the highlight of the after dinner entertainment for the conference.

We had had many rehearsals including a dummy run playing at a local Hilton Hotel but this was the song's first outing with a real audience. The song we were to perform was called *Let's Do It*.

All day I had received fabulous comments about my courage and the performance such that my confidence was bolstered like never before.

Mo introduced the song quoting Victoria Wood who said, 'This piece is a joy to perform, but a bugger to learn!' I would agree. There are six changes of key which means that you play the notes in one place to start with and it changes notes almost every time it goes up a step, becoming increasingly difficult to remember from the piano point of view.

The performance went fantastically well, we were both on absolute top form and we rocked the house down. There was still a point where I got a few notes wrong and hesitated, but we worked it into the act and the ad lib dialogue that was made up on the spot by Mo meant that no one was sure whether it was a deliberate part of the act or not.

By the end of the song the audience were banging on the tables and rolling with laughter – in the nicest possible way! Helped just a little by the free wine on the tables! It was a huge success and has been requested again and again by many delegates at conventions since that time.

Taking the initiative as I usually do, I had the event filmed for posterity and with a future goal in mind. Mo and I had talked about trying to take the performance to the Australian speaker's convention. Mo wanted to go to spend time with her sister who lived in Adelaide, and I was happy for any excuse to go back over there.

I didn't want that day to end. So many people were congratulating me and telling me what an inspiration I was up there. I felt like the star of the show. I had worked a whole year to be ready for it. When I finally went back to my room, I was so tired, but I wanted to capture how I was feeling and so wrote in my diary. The writing is a real mess. It's obvious that I was fighting sleep, but from the scrawl penned at 2.30am I was able to decipher:

I had a really FAB day. Fluffed lots but kept going. People have been coming up to me all day and saying,

'I'm so proud of you'

'You did a great job'

'I really admire you'

'Well done, you were great'

'You've transformed, you look radiant!'

What I Learnt

- It's an amazing feeling to strive for a goal over a yearlong period and reach the final winning post.

- I am braver and more courageous than I realised.

- Praise from so many people gave my confidence a massive boost.

- Mistakes if taken in your stride, can actually add great value to a performance.

- Confidence can be expanded infinitely when I really push myself beyond my comfort zone

Look out for opportunities and challenges that other people might set for you. It is only by accepting such challenges that you will have the opportunity to discover what golden talents lie beneath the surface waiting to be used. Without passion and determination to drive you forward this will be forever beyond your reach. If you haven't yet found something that fires you with that level of commitment, then consult one of the resources in the back of this book and re-read Chapter 5, 'What's the Piano in Your Life?'.

Without accepting Steve's challenge I would never have had the opportunity to discover to what extent my talents could be used. That's not just the talent to play a piano but talent in so many fundamental qualities like courage, persistence, self belief and so on. What might you be missing out on if you don't make time for such a challenge in your own life?

Disappointment

Sitting in the front row, the second day of the Professional Speakers conference, the piano no longer on the stage but tucked tightly up against the sidewall, I felt a real sense of emptiness in the pit of my stomach now that the challenge was no longer in front of me.

For so long that event had loomed so large on the horizon. I was surprised to feel so sad that my turn was over. It was like the feeling you get as a child when you've opened all your Christmas presents before 9 o'clock and there's still a whole day left to go. I had not made any plans about what next. I hadn't been able to see beyond that date.

I have felt the same sense of emptiness after many big occasions in my life. What I would like to say I have learned is always to have the next big challenge to look forward to. However, I know that I don't plan well like this. Sometimes you need to do what works for you. For me that sense of feeling proud, followed by a sense of loss, is enough to propel me into exploring what my next challenge may be.

New Goals

The next goal was to turn this experience into another opportunity. Many phone calls, e-mails and a couple of meetings later, Mo and I were on the Australian speaker's convention line-up. We were the first members from the UK association to be asked to perform over there.

Becoming an international performer felt like the best Brownie badge I had ever acquired. I could hardly believe where the journey had started and where it had ended up.

We were incredibly well taken care of and treated like stars. We had some doubts that Victoria Wood's sense of humour would travel across the continents – Australian humour is rather different from our own. We needn't have worried – the feedback after the performance was tremendous and we were recognised and stopped by many people to thank us for bringing such a piece of fun to the convention.

I still perform with Mo. Sometimes we use the songs at the end of our respective keynote presentations. In fact the whole after dinner routine has expanded into an act that stands alone with *Victoria* being followed by *Lady Lushe* – agony aunt to the stars.

If we make a mistake during a performance, it becomes a part of the act. Feeling relaxed and not knowing where the mistake will come always adds a sense of suspense that I know pays dividends. We have had people come and question us as to whether the mistakes are unintentional or indeed a part of the act. As I have mentioned before, I feel so proud that I can be so relaxed and smiling such that they are never quite sure.

It's amazing that a mistake can actually add to, not detract from a performance. I would never have thought that in the beginning, but the sense of confidence which that gives me, I find hard to express in words.

So as you expand your own abilities think big, bold and broad about how you might extend your plan and reap rewards.

At Ease with Discomfort
The practice that I had done in many locations helped me feel more at ease with the discomfort of playing in unfamiliar surroundings. I was used to feeling the symptoms of fear. I knew that it was likely that my hands would go hot and cold, I had prepared for that and knew how to combat it. I knew that it was possible that I would make a mistake, but again I had done it before and the rewards outweighed the fear. I knew that I was taking a bold stance in my life and that it was right to carry on.

Fear of Making a Mistake
Making a mistake had been one of my biggest concerns. Actually making them and coming out the other side without the world collapsing, gave me the courage to carry on to do more. In fact, even though I have now performed in public on many occasions either playing piano as a solo piece or using it as part of a speaking performance, I am still aware that it is possible that something may go wrong. However, it is only a small blip, I will not be ridiculed for it, and I have a message that is more important to get across than safeguarding my fear of failure.

There are times in my presentation when I use those mistakes to talk about how fear of such events can hold us back and what is to be gained by facing that head on.

Feeling proud

My immediate feeling after playing a piano for other people is always one of pride – feeling very proud that I have come so far. Performing in that first concert with my parents in the audience was, for me, vindication of all the past times that I had caused disappointment by not being able to fulfil their request to play for them. It had cost me in terms of conflict with them as a child. The lack of confidence in my ability under pressure had also, ultimately, cost me my piano when they sold it with the reasoning 'You never play it for us anyway!'

Many of my character traits were either abolished or seriously enhanced for me to be able to challenge my fear head on. It has left me with a much stronger repertoire of skills to call on than I ever thought would be the case. In fact, I didn't even consider the consequences of my actions when I took on the challenge. I just knew that I could no longer settle for 'one day I'm going to play a piano again.'

What's the piano in your life?

Within the borders of your comfort zone you will only ever know what you already know about yourself. It is only by stretching your ability beyond your fear of failure that you will really find the true level of your potential. There comes a time when you have to trust yourself and launch up to the next level. As the saying goes – jump and the net will appear!

Be aware that what you might initially judge as a 'mistake' can be the icing on the cake that allows your unique qualities to shine through IF you are willing to trust yourself. The level of what you are able to achieve will grow in direct proportion to the size of the strides you have the courage to take.

Summary

- Make sure you have variety in how you challenge yourself.

- Make a note of what you learn as you break through each barrier.

- Take that learning and use it when you step up to your next challenge.

- Once you have momentum, ride the crest of the wave and keep going!

- Trust yourself!

- Reward and acknowledge yourself!

- Think BIG! Think about what else you could do with this expanded ability.

- Put your learning to the test – Face the Music and WIN!

11 ... and Finally, What I Take With Me Into The Future

The skills I polished learning how to play a piano in public not only equipped me to play a piano, but also provided me with my own blueprint for success. Not only for conquering fear and stepping outside my comfort zone, but it also showed me what I need to do to produce my most focused and resourceful self. When faced with any situation that causes me to feel distracted or to feel fear, I know that I have many successful resources to call on to help me to succeed. At times this can be really frustrating when I feel a bit stuck on an issue, knowing that I should be able to work it out. I have only to ask myself what strategies I know, and how many of them am I not using, to come up with suggestions that enable me to make progress.

Sometimes though, it is only when I get back to one of my passions in which I lose myself, such as playing the piano, dancing, or horse riding, that I gain insight and answers to a current challenge.

I've learned a huge amount from my experiences – some things were new, some were relearned and reinforced. Learning how to face and conquer my fear felt like breaking free of chains that had held me back - reminiscent of releasing the catch on the Jack-in -the-box toy I used to play with as a child.

There are many things that I really value from my journey to the concert platform ...

Courage

I have proved to myself again and again that I can work towards and be successful at anything - even that which mentally and physically terrifies me. When I feel fear in an area of my life now, I can no longer accept the version of me that would, in the past, have turned her back to look elsewhere. I know that, if I put the strategies in the book to work, I will succeed.

Confidence

... in my abilities and in my sense of determination. If I work at a plan and ask for help in the right places, I know I can achieve my goals. I also know that there must be a motive that is really important to me, or a great passion burning for me to be willing to give it my time, commitment and focus.

Willingness to Make Mistakes

I have proved to myself that even when I make mistakes the learning that comes out of them far outweighs any discomfort I feel. Giving speaking presentations feels easy compared to the fear that I faced playing a piano for others the first few times.

Peace

I feel at peace with myself knowing that I am in control of my destiny. I know that I have choices about how I react to what happens in life. I have my own proven strategies of how to deal with and beat the challenges I face in my life.

Having seen what I am capable of, I know that I can turn the volume of my life up or down depending on the actions that I take. I know that it's OK to rest and be comfortable, so long as that comfort doesn't turn to stagnation. That's when I get bored, frustrated and happiness eludes me.

Belief

I believe that if I put in the effort, I can achieve almost anything I choose.

There are still some ingrained beliefs that I am working on and I am sure that this learning will never be over.

Commitment

I am committed to a life of continual learning, embracing possibility and living life to its fullest potential.

The Unexpected Results

Some things surprised me – and although unexpected, were very welcome. Don't underestimate the power of the unexpected.

Opportunities and A Mission In Life

I've been able to develop a career in speaking to inspire others to follow their own version of a piano challenge and step outside their comfort zone to discover greater potential. I never expected this as I set about my quest.

Live your dream, don't dream your life! continues to be my most frequently requested presentation.

As a direct result of listening to one of my presentations or talking to me people have done all sorts of amazing things; bought pianos, started businesses, booked long-promised holidays, quit smoking, started dance classes, created netball teams and so much more. It's a great feeling to be the spark of inspiration that leads to action in someone else's life.

My aspirations around playing a piano in public continue, and to this day, I still honour my vow to play a piano wherever I see one. This is not to boast about what I can do, but more to keep providing myself with current evidence that I can do it.

Having proved my own potential beyond fear, I am determined to make these insights, strategies and techniques available to as many people as I can, so that they too can unlock their passion and potential.

All of the above are available in some shape or form for you too. It really doesn't require a visit to the Wizard of Oz to find your courage; all it takes is finding your passion and doing something about it!

My Request Of You

Speak Up and Get Some Help

I would like to help you on your journey of self-discovery. Let me know what it is that you want to achieve and I will help you in whatever way I can. Contact me via my web site to tell me how you are doing with YOUR challenges and goals. I'd love to know what you took away from this book that made a difference.

Six Degrees of Separation
My quest is to share my story and strategies with as many other people as I can.

What companies and organisations do you know who would want to hear presentations based on the content of this book?

Who do you know who would benefit from a copy of this book?

Please contact me via my web site: tracy@tracyplaice.com

May you flourish when you face your own music and win!

Good luck with your quest!

Tracy Plaice

Resources

To find resources mentioned in the book, such as questions to help you put together your plan of action, tables to chart your progress, and audio versions of the listed exercises, visit www.tracyplaice.com

Other resources mentioned in this book ...

Conquering Fear
Feel the Fear and Do It Anyway. Susan Jeffers. Dutton

Fearless Living. Rhonda Britten. Hodder and Stroughton

Fearless Loving. Rhonda Britten. Hodder and Stroughton

Fight Your Fear and Win. Don Green. Random House

Keeping Your Nerve. Kate Jones. Faber

The Confident Performer. David Roland. Currency Press Ltd and Nick Hern Books Ltd

Positively Fearless. Vera Peiffer. Out of print, but keep an eye out in the second hand bookshops – that's where I got my copy

DO IT! John-Roger and Peter McWilliams. Prelude Press

The Psychology of Achievement. Brian Tracy (Tape series)

Musical Performance

The Inner Game of Music. Barry Green and Tim Gallwey. Pan Books

Piano Notes. Charles Rosen. The Penguin Group

Dominic Alldis, Jazz Pianist, Conductor and Motivational Speaker. www.musicandmanagement.com

Finding Your Passion

Find Your Passion. Jo Parfitt. Summertime Publishing
What Color Is Your Parachute? Richard Nelson Bolles. Ten Speed Press

The Artist's Way. Julia Cameron. Pan McMillan

Dealing with Emotion

How to Stop Worrying and Start Living. Dale Carnegie. Reed Consumer Books Ltd

The Happiness Project. Robert Holden. www.happiness.co.uk

Relationship Issues

Too Good to Leave, Too Bad to Stay. Mira Kirshenbaum. The Penguin Group

The Art and Science of Love. John Gottman and Julie Schwartz. www.gottman.com

Creative Thinking

The Magic of Thinking Big. David Schwartz. Simon & Schuster, Inc

The Mind Gym. Octavius Black and Sebastian Bailey. Time Warner. www.themindgym.com

Coaches / NLP Practitioners / Professional Speakers

Mo Shapiro. NLP Trainer, Motivational Speaker, After dinner entertainer. www.inform-global.co.uk

Michael Tipper. Accelerated Learning, speed-reading, memory techniques. www.positivelymad.co.uk

Keith Banfield. Sales and Marketing Coach. www.plusresults.com

Martin Carver. www.a-gconsulting.com

Gerard Jakimavicius. www.life-coach-associates.com

Barefoot Lifecoaching. Offer a great training option with University accreditation if you are interested in becoming a life coach. Also there are a limited number of free coaching sessions available from people who are training as part of the programme. www.barefootcoaching.co.uk. www.coachingcircle.co.uk/free.php

UK College of Hypnosis and Psychotherapy. www.coaching-life.co.uk/pages/resources-hyp.htm

Nutrition
The Optimum Nutrition Bible. Patrick Holford. Piatkus Books Ltd. www.patrickholford.com

Eating for Peak Performance. Rosemary Stanton. Allen and Unwin

The Juice Master's Ultimate Fast Food. Jason Vale. Thorsons

Enhancing Brain Function
Henry Hopking of Life Systems International. www.life-systems.org

Aromatherapy
The Fragrant Pharmacy. Valerie Ann Worwood. Bantam

On-line Networking Groups
Ecademy. www.ecademy.co.uk

Magenta Circle. www.magentacircle.co.uk

Linked-In. www.linkedin.com

Speaking Resources

Toastmasters. www.toastmasters.org

Professional Speakers Association.
www.profressionalspeakers.org (UK)
www.nationalspeakers.org.au (Australia)
www.nsaspeaker.org (America)

Web Site Content/Copy Editing

Angela Sherman, Content Creation.
www.content-creation.co.uk

Printed in the United Kingdom
by Lightning Source UK Ltd.
113365UKS00001B/61-270